Conversations
With Angels

Collected Poems

Brian Kirk Moilanen

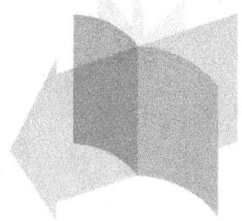

Chapbook Press

Schuler Books
2660 28th Street SE
Grand Rapids, MI 49512
(616) 942-7330
www.schulerbooks.com

Conversations With Angels

ISBN 13: 9781966196419

Library of Congress Control Number: 2025921924

Trust is a key ingredient

Trust is a key ingredient
Within a deplorable assessment of unbiased belief
Once upon the forthright-when assessed
It can equal as words of gold and be revealing within a relief
Yet often times it takes momentarily to test the water
Possibly lead by and with example
For when you tug vigorously
Often times this will keep you in mind-you must also pull
Is a leader or a boss of significance made or born
Speaking objectively
This can be argued either as victory or even as folklore
Make efforts to not only only take-but also to give
Emotions run rampant that sometimes will leak as a sieve
Testing the water(s)
Sometimes is it a necessity to be strict and conservative
Sometimes it is superlative to carry on as without doubt-very bright?
But now tedious and bright being hmm...swift and polite
Without the night and darkness Is there also just a black light?
Furthermore-without mistakes just how is it to learn?
And not only a test of wills-but just why ever fight?
Not taking a risk is a risk in itself
That would be like a Christmas without red stockings or even Santa's giving elf
A profusion of supplies
Hmm...even deeper what about the need for a supply shelf?
Educating within a reaction or an action of what an idea might get
The Lord will accept you as you are
Significant news
That is heard from an angels voice and travel very far
Quitters just won't win
And henceforth-winners just won't quit
If you don't make efforts to win
Becoming complacent with losing you won't be a hit
Try and try again
Don't throw in the towel
Something about oppression is both greedy and foul
Honor your elders
Give interest to all
The world does not revolve around only you
If you do you are shallow and despondent
And your friends with luckily more than just two
Give a new hobby a chance
If you fail-you can honestly say that you did try
My conscious is free
And furthering with the attention given to-more than just comply
There is know reason to lie
Just do not deny

WRITTEN BY:BRIAN MOILANEN-2023

A narcissus nature

You have formed a superfluous pleasant term admiring
An inner beauty with bountiful prestige of great looks
Guard off with these hands wonderfully in process of
Warding away any dishonor that will maybe capture any crooks
Keeping what is right and also mention rightfully mine
And not to mention all that I have worked for and also against
Forgiveness comes in the method of tried efforts to amend
And yes-even though trivial spiritually this soul repents
You carry yourself with diligence upon every stride
When and if the understanding of a dream will be applied
I will defeat any conspiracy or collusion and let the plane comfortably glide
As you know the balance of heaven and hell do and will collide
Sometimes this battle is lopsided and the challenger must stand
I won't give in or give up and let you become full of a menacing malice
I don't have an owners manual
Nor do I believe that any soul does
A flurrying display of emotion amplitude
Thanks for the antidote and also its buzz
Carry on with virtue
Give in to this cliche exemplifying good moral worth
More names written into the Lambs book of life
Thank heavens for your infant and the totality of pleasant birth
A win today
Adding up with a win tomorrow
Action along with good news
Defeat the ever present neighboring sorrow
If it looks like a car
And toots like a car
Hmm....more than likely ...it is a car
What comes of heredity and DNA and also RNA?
Two ends of the spectrum
Spirits and angels know that morality unfortunately do play
Do blood lines of lineage make the story complete?
Superb rendition just won't allow for two left feet
Won't it?
Or Will it?
A product of environment
And there is not one blood type specifically found
Sometimes maybe I am a little bit brash
And with exception aside-sometimes systems will and also do clash
A narcissistic nature
Just whom and what defines this nomenclature?
Refined and polished
A shining star
I define myself and allow the you to define the you
You then in turn are rehearsing in quality and assurance...
The goodness of the substance of two
For even in church the center stage finds all of us
As we are in the proper isle and not to mention also the proper pew
WRITTEN BY: BRIAN MOILANEN 2022

A place in which to turn

Where do I turn when it appears that all I do turns south?
I try to defeat the odds at all cost
Yet it is obvious that today as the yesterday is confused by your damning mouth
A place in which to turn
A gathering possibly noticing that I will win
Consistent with not ever giving in
I feel as if turmoil itself gets beaten and could even be a sin
Christianity attempts to withhold
Am I growing younger in virtue or just concealing truth and getting old?
Am I actually my own worst enemy?
I attest to saying my own brain gets wiser in efforts that do scold
The temperature gets lukewarm
Yet I know that 10 below zero is truly very cold
It is a mass illusion
A mind confusion
A twisting of the brain
Going into a loss
That gets repeated into a sustenance of refrain
Good friends
Acknowledging that enemies are also there
Stack up on the playing cards
These days why does a loss entertain as a friend or constant foe?
I am not burning the candle on both ends
Yet in patterns I cry for all
My heart of desperation screams
A symbol
A goal-the need for more
A game of cards so
That is won and lost by what begins to show
A game face
That even when losing is never too low
We all enter the earth-alone
Surrounded by and with family
A very consistent overture
Spoken in soft and subtle temperance-call this overtone
Will you be there for me?
If I put on the blinders temporarily
And change my mind at any cost
Will you help?
Will you hold my hand?
Time thru an hourglass
Excessive in time-Too much sand
I cannot give up
I cannot give in
I cannot quit
I have to play my hand
Even though I don't want to
God and his presence is obvious
And the emphasis is forever
What a speed
As the days and time pass
I want to survive and caste out the impure
A game although at confusion
I will win-that is for sure

WRITTEN BY:BRIAN MOILANEN-2022

A proclamation of peace-not of fists

Hold back from blatant hostility
Find and locate a method of peaceful assembly
Thanks for the catering of you to me
A real situation of zero cost and abiding to more than a few
Love will find and henceforth peace shall follow suite
Words that tend to break only sabotage the innocent and pure soul
In lay-men's terms this one time instance will not defile or pollute
A proclamation of peace-not of fists
To my God I raise the militant salute
This crafty awareness understands too full length authority given
And with tactics of obligation this tried heart resists
Life is a test for all
Honesty wins as being my practice that evidently exists
Hang onto truth of all situation and let chaos take the fall
Words that tend to excite
Others that musingly may perplex
Bless your enemies to alleviate prolonged sadness of disorder
Read and reread this text to remove any vile hex
Win and be right with God
Do your homework of gathered goodness
Allowing peace in a world that finds this statement as odd
Believe
Achieve
Apply this salve to destroy what others
Claim that you will not ever relieve
Speak not necessarily in contrast of situations that console
Or maybe not absorb as is borrowed being a metaphor
Open the heart
And open the windows of the soul
Throw the dice in anticipation...
Or or you dismantled to see 7's on the luck of nearly every roll
What comes around
Obviously goes around
Be free as often as possible
A soldier that was once lost-is now happily found

WRITTEN BY:BRIAN MOILANEN-2020

A unique blend of the generic

I don't play
I yet also must say it can be difficult to bend
I am with tension added-engaged into the facades of reacting
Those of us on bowed and bent knees although do pray-methods in which to readily mend
Forgive
Forget
Move forward
Raise the ante and place hope of winning the long shot delivered spiritual bet
Yea
Yea
Can't you give the balancing act of sight and soul a deserved smile-no regret
Some say to please those that please you
Confrontation can sour a situation-trials and tribulation we all will get
How about the foot trades that of your shoe
A unique blend of the generic
The splash of sweet spirited wine-angels defeat demons yet the battle is firm
I am playing my hand to the likes with passion and will not allow time to plunder and fret
A new day that we arise enveloping brilliant sunshine
Is already sometimes a God given win
Lead by example and use motive of love
To transpire into an earnest and happy grin
I am setting my sights quite high
Giving to the needy puts my soul and heart in a sacred place
I cannot argue or even with my conscious alarmed ever although deny
Skies of blue
Clouds of white
God is my anchor on the sea of madness
And heals even those that only have the faith of a mustard seed
I am not flashy
What I own is surely not the best
Yet what I have apparently will do the job
I along with my friends and foes will retire solemnly into a night of rest
It is okay to be meek
Be of this world yet oddly enough-also different
Those that play and use malice beit that of evil
Will locate the King now or on their death bed
Good day and never blame the King
Teach the world the Holy Bibljjje as in the heavens I hear angels sing

WRITTEN BY BRIAN MOILANEN-2020

Acknowledging the Creator

Acknowledging the Creator
A step that I endure and always do pursue
All things evident as of now
In what method of madness-Can I put the propriety together to stick as super glue?
What path to take
And what about the effectiveness of others-some are angels of choice
Follow the God Almighty-For this Grande Entity of love will automatically see you thru
Do not cheat
Do not provoke
The efforts at hand are reconciliation of good-and not substantiated with the need of recreational weed
No marijuana needed-no green smoke
No life so short where the cards are stacked and seemed to be within any type of defeat
Learn about the Maker to be obtain the Upper Seat
Do not perpetuate into any malice beit ill will
A hard life lived-yet I am happy still
Step out of your own soul
See the path of God and his Son Jesus Christ
Do not steal or rob
My advice-stay way from the paradox of a manifested and sickening bank heist
Get off your behind
Take a stand as a figure of speech without disregard
Pray for an answer and let go of it all
And walk with frolic throughout the green courtyard
A time to believe
A time to serve
If I get on your bad-side
It is not my effort to unnerve
Take a look into the beyond
Take a glance into what is deep
Bye God-Somehow the opposition will win
Sometimes it's you versus your fate of God-Somehow
The easier path is yours
My effort is to abstain from unruly antiquity-call it sin
A kid with passion shops for candy in grocery stores
The parents engage within joy
The children smile
The planet earth make friends with substance-a relevancy of time that on occasion will annoy
Or does it make your infant smile?
A winning path
Within that obtaining a clandestine leisure style
The youth shall win
The man of tin
Add it all up
And learn the substance of humility
To gather humbly as a Challis incorporating your eternal way
Do you know what I mean?
Do you hear what I imply by these words that I do say?
Follow the King of Kings
For this entity of Grande gives you choice
The candle may burn at both ends
But loyalty wins as the heart bends

WRITTEN BY:Brian Moilanen-2024

An angelic answer

You are now being endorsed to being my holy angel
Words comprehend into a complete love
With sentence structures that permeate as to a prodigy that does tell
Dreams and inspiring traditions that are immortal to most
I sip on my black warm coffee that lights this morning ritual
And eat slowly my heavily buttered and tasty strawberry flavored toast
Love
Love
Surrounded by diamond and silver mansions
Streets of gold
Clouds resemble gigantic pictures of Christ and ultimately-Jehovah God
Not forgetting to mention also the work of messenger angels
That cure persons always
And reverse what was thought of as irreversible spells
No way to disregard with concurrent wins
I pray on upon my bended knee and consequently also my bodies shins
Stories quite sublime and sort of-like being both new and old
Moses taught the masses the doctrines of Christ
The chapters concur with pages that maybe are usually manifested with being sold
Random acts of kindness
Be courteous and do your best
A heart on trial is a solemn instigation of evil men's fire
He should not although work for his maker
He is ill-pray for him-for he fashions himself as being an undertaker
Whispers although are heard as freedom-the angels have confessed
Walk the line being the undeniable test
Restitution
Pray and pray alike
Entering into a saintly area
Also understood as being the human psyche
The Good Lord
Evidently-He both does sometimes give
And other times He will take
He will guide you a within a safe path
He will wash both your heart, soul, and mind
A civilian soldier is beyond fair
And he will work for good of humanity-He has not always been
A fighter-a lover of souls is what he truly is…and completely fair
The Lord steers to stray from sin
For you and I-not always easy- quite a task
Yet if you follow your heart-each day can be a win
A meaning that never ceases to amaze or create a solution
The movie that you are viewing is coming to its beginning-you are now more complete
Heaven is somewhere between paradise and other ethereal worlds
You will have a better tomorrow
Christ will dry your tears
And undue any and all past sorrow

WRITTEN BY:BRIAN MOILANEN-2024

<u>**Angels**</u>
Angels protect
Angels provide
Angels with ease solve problems
Just observe what they provide
Wow-can turn heart-ache into joy
And with consecrated power-turn swinging fists into peace
Sometimes we all grow weary and become weak
But I hope and aim to reach deepening solace
And as with my advice granted-turn the screw into a release
It is often said that these angels of our Lord carry on being His messengers
But don't let down your guard for what now is technically only to appease
Action being into that of uniquely to pacify and calm
Let go of panic to test your ability to resolve
Speaking to angels and spirits from up above is my subject at hand
I pray for heaven all around to enter my heart and turn to revolve
Common sense liturgy fashions my tenure-draw a line in the sand
Christian rules placate into what our God does hate
Sin and inequities our Lord and Maker put forth efforts for that to be banned
Find time to pray
I hope this enters your conscious as utmost true
I suspect that you are gathering stronger-I imagine that you hear what I say?
Talking with an earthly angel is my goal
Finding both your heart and also your divinity of soul
Christian rock and roll
I am under the bridge only twice-if you know what I mean
It is great to see see and like-wise also be seen
I will pay the toll
Cling and adhere to Christ as being the King of Kings
Also the Lord of Lords
The Maker of such things has spirits with him always
Within always
Rendering with as always within
Detour your heart from inequities
Turn from ever present sin
God will always come into your character early
And tending to that never be late
Gambling with love and content heart
Salvation will envelope as a newer choice and/or fate
Turn form hate
Make note to arrive on time and not be late

WRITTEN BY:BRIAN MOILANEN-2024

ARCADIAN

I hope that you are feeling both good and true
And this understanding goes beyond yourself
This definition reveals itself as not much more than arcadian
This simpleness of contentment forms a unique solid glue
I hope that this joy of personage stays on this testing track
Whispering sentiments of hmm..good luck to these fateful few
Some say this subtle feeling nears euphoria
Shining light like the sun and night intervenes with the glowing full moon
In spite of it being high noon occasionally I laugh at the world around me
And as my senses remain together I adhere with silly actions such as a buffoon
A one way pass to heaven
Is this what today and forever hold in hand?
This being an intrinsic command
A supplemental demand?
Is this surreal feeling part of my gene pull?
Or merely a focus centered on how I play my cards?
Or even invisible holy angels that act as superlative guards?
Philosophy to some
Which to some may appear as objective
Or to others a mainstay which occurs as parallel of objective
Others seem to be more diligent
We all sin against our Maker and his hosts
But turn this around and bring with you all your smiles
The trip is long and
May take a hundred years or so and be further than anything, a million miles
Open doors
Yet remain true and legitimate
Theses cards may not be what you wanted
But play them you must
Inspirations all from God and his living testaments and even testimony
For in God we trust
And not viewed as being phony
Be part of the team
Or be part of the cause
Living life on lives terms can bring its cuts but we have the gauze
Treating the conscious and brain nearly the same
We all have our feelings
And if any demons were ever found without angst we must tame
The mad scientist is currently baffled with his own cause
Hypnotized
Bewildered by the essence of what's truly real
Molecular motion
Unrecognized chemicals and their undying devotion
One mans ocean
Could be another mans puddle of mud
Essentials that cannot be omitted
And thrown aside to the garbage amid all the crud
Tens of gallons verse a trillions of gazillions
Take and know that love is within all hearts
Be brave and know that this life may seem quite long
Play the record again to hear this bold and significant song

WRITTEN BY:BRIAN MOILANEN-spring of 2022

Armed with anger

My mind is still-not yet free
Attempting to beat the flagrant odds
Yet strangely enough with accurate vision still yet do see
Mental warfare triggers this trouble for all undying ages
To coming crashing down within my angry and restless soul
As we all do know- empty pockets lean towards penny less sages
Armed with anger
But uniquely enough I do not own a gun with bullets
Plagued and juggling grief-the instrument of danger
Stepped on in many ways that would endanger this scarlet heart
Obtained excellence with compassion equals as solace within
And in many ways without-my mouth instantly becomes a sour tart
Working to create the newest holy angels
Give luck of the draw a non discriminatory earnest chance
Watch the angels looking within
As my heart is immersed with pristine red wine creating a spiritual dance
Seeing and observing
Observing and seeing
More readily spoke about good news
Do you now notice that your brain partners this prayer-and you too also are agreeing?
This is not a delusion
This also is not a hallucination
Faith heals this anomaly of any confusion
Hang tight and stay having acquired angelic conversation
Interestingly both properties unite appearing as a fusion
Give this tried heart a break so you may be healed to leave the hospital or institution
And furthering this salutation of a letter I wrote it strays from being a visual illusion
...And furthermore I am sure my patriotic leanings include me within the Constitution
I ultimately recognize that immediately
I have earned an easy shot at an understandable restitution
My ambitions are running dry and heartaches take a toll
Going this fast forward but the great times I hope to with confidence rewind
I am fortunate although on the other hand
Bestowed with a Godly instinct-and also am not blind
Like a young docile child who grows and has a wonderful mind
Do your letter writing to Jehovah and answers you will find
The inner growl subsides
My human psyche takes a break
Taming the wild lion within
Aiming to please and likewise to be pleased
Heck...this disturbance of self alone almost seems a cardinal sin

WRITTEN BY:BRIAN MOILANEN-2020

Backbone

Petrified within angst we hear the people scream
Henceforth others begin to blatantly yell
Another fortunate soul is freed with the cross of Christ
The story narrated by the holy angel reveals good versus evil so much to tell
Be bold and learn to give respect
Live free and don't ever neglect
This salvation happens haphazardly and pays virtue to justice
A train that stays on the tracks and that has not wrecked
Backbone
For most grows stronger through progress of time
If you can't fall in love
Find that defeating venting frustration comes with an uphill climb
Emotions
Feelings
Response to whatever the sentiment or situation brings
Where is the guarantees of youth and adult and everything in between?
A lifetime of living as we all acquire purpose and testament that clings
Heart of a champion
Not forgetting to mention failures which we all can attest to
Sometimes and rarely winners do quit
Yet beat the odds and watch the world of yours take shape-adhesive is the glue
Persevere
Wait out the storm
Don't allow the end too get much too near
Turn from any gut-wrenching fear
Feel sunshine on these shoulders and actually feeling very warm
Endure
A test for all a also not discriminating between person to person
A time that knowingly we are stuck between run and walk
This undeniable measure Is too just crawl
Strength in character
I at one time was pushed to the side
No longer will I put up with being taken for granted
I will follow all my lengthy protocol and continue to abide
Your hysterical and wild behavior supplies an idiot convention-all ranted
Stay put together
Loose the outdoor weather that flies high as a two ton feather

WRITTEN BY:BRIAN MOILANEN-2020

Better days will follow
You have taken quite earnestly
Your fair share of hits
I have a heart and truly do feel for you
And I do wonder-is this one size fits all shoe?
Dabbling with madness and with hindsight of madness
For as any other mused in between, not sure if I sense peaches or pits
Menaced with and without all the evil that so many own and possess
For heavens sake you must take a stand
Open these portals and doors of brilliance and begin to bless
Pick all of your battles wisely
Neglect what you can't encompass and say so long to all that stress
Victory eventually will be yours
Glancing at my watch goodness will plainly confess
Once a baby and their birth is born
Patterns of success and the like are noticed and also noted
Keep in prayer that none have become forlorn
Or that an abundance of sadness ever fits it suit with emotions of seeing red
The gods will steer you straight and probably never scorn
Two sides of the coin to choose from
And don't be disturbed and become torn
Although even in that trend of uncertain desire
A gallon of water to put out the raging fire
A brand new car compares with empty feelings and a flat tire
Reviewing my life I am not sure of what is greater
Fate or free will
Aspirins and their counterpart-both those intentions of a pain kill
Within all brains and souls
You will locate a library full of trepid thought
For a battle that is won is not always a battle that was fought
Wins
Losses
You can't discount more-over even the ties
For if this life brings great happiness
Is there truly much needed to add understanding that we all need to revise?
Better days will follow
Sometimes in the treacherous oceans of life
We must purchase or borrow
Take a stand
For this might be your calling card
Your actions are observed and you may see an angry you might be barred
A way out
Also a way in
A summers day
Eventually could lead to a win
And also a compass to forthright bring direction
I am a a lone wolf at times and I also need affection
We all have want
We all have need
A nation at war is the nation that will and does bleed
Get today the daily news
Forgive me for any problems that in the past that I may have caused
Don't fuss
Try to get over even mistakes of your choosing
If not'
The essence of your soul you might be losing
Better days will follow
Better days now and always will follow
My heart is immersed with good
And no longer hollow

WRITTEN BY:BRIAN MOILANEN-2022

Birds and beasts

Birds and beasts
Refuge must quickly be taken within another situation
Serving the King I am allured by both the righteous ordained pastors and priests
Yet the enemies are present among the fickle crowd-a menacing determination
Some view this as a detriment for all mankind-a decline in thanksgiving and family feasts
Fight or flight
What choice will render way of decision?
Souls equipped accordingly to either propaganda-walk by faith and not by sight
And as for me-I will make my own revision
With no suspicion of division
Certain battles are without end
Universal efforts march forward peacefully
God gives you the options protocol and much more to lend
Some straight paths begin to bend
And some bent paths begin to straighten up
Drink the potion of red wine from the sacrificial challis
Albeit also known in majesty and forgiveness the golden Christ cup
When do lives battles slow down or end?
Time is on your side
Buckle up for the ride
Problems protest yet eventually also subside
I myself follow the Lord and am entrenched without war currently-I shall abide
Do my best to not turmoil and not let the two components ever collide
Thou shalt have no other God's before me
Life is a freely given gift and when in a sinful nature
I aim to modify and be readily fulfilled too also repent
A substance of this understanding allows me to be confident and candidly sure
Jesus saves and is sure to have been heaven sent
Time through an hourglass
And at a glance inside I know that the sand just cannot be with dent
Configurations that always make sense
And therefore I do gratefully acknowledge
And in amazement I almost get pulled in-as if a mud stuck in uniquely thick and dense
I make a vow to serve only good
And like wise-good will locate my path
God is love
Yet turn your back on him-then you must beware for his jealous wrath
Clean your character and soul
In layman's terms please give it a cleansing and pure ordained bath

WRITTEN BY:BRIAN MOILANEN-2020

Blessed if you do

Blessed if you do
Blessed if you don't
Mercy granted if you will
Mercy granted if you won't
Not to mention an exact emotion for everything under the sun
Retribution will find all
And if weighed might just equal that of a ton
Sad and mad
Glad and bad
What does all of this mean?
Further more what to subtract and henceforth what to add?
Traveling the earth with a just reason
Traveling still as I write-that of a nomad
Obedience
Follow the protocol of your mission
Are or have you experienced the belief of supernatural events and beings?
This touches the mind uniquely and harvests superstition
Declaration of Lineage
For example your folklore of family tree is good
Or is it great?
Or is it nil and much too late
Within all of us runs a bloodline
Using metaphors as a method of accuracy
Choices evidently concur with RNA and DNA and also chromosomes
For that matter-what is your blood type?
Is it as follows...
A
B
AB
or...O?
Using directed humor-some say I'm negative
But they're not positive
Proteins and antigens divide the flow of blood to the brain and everywhere else
Follow at any rate
Your own particular path
Clean up your ways
And cleanse the soul and body with sudsy bath
Pay extra attention to play it smart
Yet confused I am as my new car
Just keeps on coming vehemently apart
Once again emotions back in the mix
I fold and cross my arms with this crucifix
The magician although won't reveal all of his tricks

WRITTEN BY:BRIAN MOILANEN-2020

Breaking the bank

I did it again
I did not live within my means
A trigger of my obsessive self
Or even from there-what happens behind the scenes
Spending gazillions on self, family, and friends
A holy testimony so to say
And the plot thickens and takes it's moderate bends
Addicted to money
Subscribing to cash
Maybe hold a party
Maybe as odd as it seems-have a bash
Subsidizing to monetary values
Or lack of...I usually hurry and strangely enough also do dash
I sit on my couch reviewing all these events taken place
I am different
But still one within this fast paced human race
Like a detective I won't let the guilty run and hide
For they will not leave without a trace
I am fair, just, and impartial
If desired
You may leave me in your will
If not-a battle won
Is undeniably a battle fought
And likewise the same as a young kid in a candy store
Look at the goodies that he has bought
Or analytically put
Look at all that was deserved and also taught
Money equals to cash
A fiscal dollar
Monetary attributes
Monetary substitutions and zero disputes
If the sky rained money
And all houses worth gold, silver, and bronze
This is becoming my discernment
For I ask forgiveness
And cannot deny-I also repent
What if I was worth all of the tea in China
I suppose this much is over the top
Like drinking rum and soda
You gather what I mean-I am speaking of liquor and pop
But I must remember this much
Money cannot buy me love
But-it creates options and choice of choices
Do you see redemption and peace
And the flight of the white holy dove
I have heard it said sometimes hobbies can be an addiction
Henceforth
...And so on
I always try with whatever there is to do
Comforted affidavit
A winning touch of perception locates the proper fitting shoe

WRITTEN BY:BRIAN MOILANEN-2022

Bright and brand new world
Systemic intervals

Just what is what and whom are the fools?

Staying committed to freedom

And none the less why we go to schools

Education is a driving force to lead and give guidance to a desiring soul

Pencil and notebook in hand

For these items are now my tools

Do all needed to attain rigid flexibility

Occurrences sustain equating while seeing no one is truly odd

We are basically all the same in more ways than one

No need to examine me or others as I am one in whom you cannot prod

Somedays melancholy spins my mind whipping in circles

Two sides of the coin and both sides take the center of my aura

Bright and brand new world

Euphoria equates to the pinnacle of a good mental intrigue

Am I all alone

Did I form upon my observation a changing of the tide?

Don't give up

Think a win every day that passes

Stockpile on the paradox of what was taught

Also stockpile on individual success

Inner clocks

Interest is instructing my brain and heart to do the winding

Inner clocks

Better days to follow and we are once again finding

Today a great day

Tomorrow I will hold in high esteem

The sun is tucked behind the clouds while it also winks at me between the skies

Formidable and tested

I if need be will and shall keep on board and not be in disguise

A soul with attitude on high yet not superior or a proud soul

Humble ways are what I have devised

WRITTEN BY: BRIAN MOILANEN-JUNE 2022

Climbing in hate

Are you falling in love?
Or are you climbing in hate?
So much is predictable
Yet none the less-mercy although probably will wait
Advised by my friends to only do my best
Maybe a cup of hot coffee and Biblical reading shall revise this text
A symptom of understood problems I need
To be blessed and to bless both enemy and neighbor-this is a test
The expenditure of saving my soul and spirit-to move forward with God speed
Climbing in hate-we have all been there before
Do your homework steadfast
To complete a never-ending chore
The winds above do blow from sea to sea
As they stretch apart the earth-and also the skies to prove what is in store
Anger and loathing
To detest and dislike
Elements that create emotions and feelings too
Weighing in both statistics of the human psyche
I must obey my Maker to learn just what is right
A parable
A quest of infinite whirlwind
I to have done what is wrong-For we all have sinned
A common ground for us all
I am speaking with a heart of stalemate and consistent understanding
Quite demanding-breaking through with...
What this heart of desire clings and is also demanding
What is commanding?
Try to locate and esteem what is right
Follow your heart
Follow your personal God and also your guide
Hop on in
And make effort to enjoy this ride
Take things with a grain of salt-and move together as one
Work and effort are consistent to being their own reward
Take time to also enjoy the radiant warm sun
Play sweet music and work with the proper chord
Give praise when it is due
Friends are abundant as I answer to both the me and also the you
I hope that I have centered in on this common strife
Bye the way-have you ever heard the term that...
If you have a happy life-henceforth you will have a happy life?
Learn to acquire
Also acquire to learn
Heaven and hell are consistent with the doxology
Of don't play with fire or you two could just eternally burn
Win the war through your fervent desire
And complete this with that of creating to what is now my turn

WRITTEN BY:BRIAN MOILANEN-2024

Deciphering between blessings and curses

What is a blessing to one
May just be s curse to another
How to move forward with eloquence itself?
Christmas customs prove although that is not just awkward instance
Hearts and stockings become filled with joy by Santa's elf
And through blessings we do have a christian sister or brother
Memories remain on your presiding life shelf
I forfeit my own blood which spoils to another
Locating my God uniquely with graced wisdom I must add
Gifts given either spiritual or temporal-from one to the other
Condolence is equality granted beit that of happy or sad
Deciphering between blessings and curses
Hospitals cater to the sick
And evidently the doctor's care-then the hierarchy continues with abiding nurses
Retain belief
As strangely enough biblical prayer is released to raise the ante along with the purses
Folklore proves that life is a battle between good and bad
Take aim to not allow your stomach to sour
A test of tests-From intrinsic to that of mad
When burning hot fire and iced freezing cold collide
Believe in something greater than yourself
Which allows for something greater as heartaches will also subside
We all have triumph and tragedy from cradle to grave
Break on thru to the other side with spirituality in which to hide
Yet not all are we able to save
Too most of all questions we also have contradiction
A healthy infliction
Bye the way what is your view on superstition?
Or for that matter...regarding your won benediction?
Or...not to spook you but how about premonition?
Save the world
Save a soul
No money currently to my name
Yet the angels will diverse and pay my way at the toll
As you know-Jesus Christ died for all
An unjust cruel bleeding crucifixion
As for me-I admire the vigilantes who make their own jurisdiction
It is difficult to leave you with only my one focus of valediction
Drop a line to my critics who forthright have created my malediction

WRITTEN BY: BRIAN MOILANEN-2020

Detain the diabolic demise

The only thing that you did wrong is have the wrong tint or hue to your skin
Remedial preference is usually that of pallid white
You this time yet although must win
I am Caucasian uniquely yet quite accurately once again witness mankind's sin
Sin of heart
In turn leads to a heart of sickening sin
My color of clothes is that of a jet black
Yet I always get treated as if different which substantiates to an innocent label of chagrin
Okay
Okay
Yet it is tough to move forward collectively when all that you have is a tried and tested proclamation
That is always a ticking time bomb attitude-for you are the next of kin
The Almighty God in the heavens will take a stand
And sweet Jesus will shake the heavens within a fury of strong and abiding overtone
A heart that has been oppressed
Is a heart that knowingly speaks without soft or subtle temperance-a quieted moan
Call the President of public relations
And hope that he or she is candid and honest with complete relevance on the cell phone
The only wrong doing sometimes is those that do wrong to the innocent
So now the cards take a subtle turn for the best
A time for both parties to engage into goodness-a welcoming of the word repent
And help to be what the plot has just openly confessed
Lies and corruption
Cant we all just get along
The strong are the decent-yet what about the christian hope song?
Words of valor
Where went words of true disposal?
Break the hate of those that are different from you
As a matter of fact-trade the foot with your own shoe
We all have a dream
We also in accordance have a hope
Clean up your act
And lather the soul with a concoction of home made soap
WWJD
Or as it is also known to be...what would Jesus do?
One of the brave and an accredited giving people
I enjoy walking on the church pillars on foggy nights such as this
And my greatest feat is a tight rope tip toe crawl on the church steeple
Is it true that if we all give more to society and the unfortunate ones
We shall please the omnipotent and he will grant us favor?
A sweet taste accompanies my mouth
And it is very sweet

WRITTEN BY:BRIAN MOILANEN-2020

Dig in your heals

Dig in your heals
Mercy conducts
This revelation obviously reveals
You think that you have it tough
Me being a catalyst for the destitute poor-I bring forthright
Endurance and waiting out this test of living
At certain moments as this-the enemy surrounds and is surrounding me to fight
Sometime with lethal fists
Sometime with verbal onslaught-a tongue that does ravenously bite
Find your personalized playbook and book of rules with added decree
Now I am being tried in every shape with angle and form
Thank God I do see
I must
I need
I shall-I will
I ought
Pride a tough one to swallow
The test not what I thought
Sentiments not purchased by living-I am not complete yet either hallow
You can't change your illustrious meaning that they planned
A 50/50
Equations of the vast exploring of my own mind-time thru an hourglass moderate with sand
Misunderstood
Judging by sight and character read
This should be illegal-operation mind crime
This much and even more I w ill inform you and concede
Don't judge a book by it's cover
Read the book first
From Genesis to Revelations-and all other chapters in-between
This Holy book being all you need-It feeds the hunger and quenches the thirst
Pray and pray alike
Or become victim in the difficulty of the escapade
The talk of moving on without any evil is tough to acknowledge
Is this understanding true-or much more received an escapade
Do all of your spiritual homework and stay in college
War finds some
Peace abides it's path and caters to good
A fireplace that roars with fire
Is seen as amber that breeds on soft dry wood
How does the old saying and cliché go?
For me it's as simple as this...
Bring in the morning with a hot mug of sizzling black joe

WRITTEN BY:BRIAN MOILANEN-2020

Directions to love street

Hmm..Been driving for hours at what seems as if days
Comparing as rats and mice within perils of space and time
Understood to me as if trapped with obviously that of a convoluted maize
Finding corners along with curves and boundless amount of turns
What direction to take-what to leave behind and just what stays
Not feeling at all aloof-my pierced soul and spirit radically churns
Some people lose their mind but I suppose that the conscience plays
I tend to attempt to put out fires and whatever just burns
What the heart retracts is quite ridiculous-along with sacred ways
Directions to love street
Just when was your last visit there?
I am quite real and pulling no punches
A tried and true character
Brings in believers all around
Save a soul
Direction drives forward-and stability is found
Epic stories of substance contain heroes and unique similar realm
A prodigy of goodness-can you handle this testimony?
Try not to falter as you could and might overwhelm
Save the world-Also-save yourself
Chronicles explode with quality
The more you do-occasionally the more you will see
I am proud of the winners with a PHD
The overall effect
Is to try-find me even one heart that does not agree?
I feel so to say-as being on Saint street
Locations being found
Are you free?
And move together as quite relevant-and advance forward-The trumpets will sound
Obtaining love
Securing abundance of hope
I recall as a lad-with a drunken sailors mouth-my folks made me taste soap
Yet this strengthened me and made me as complete
Paving paths of serenity and not even smoking dope
Maybe cherish those bountiful days and times as earning a heavenly seat
If you follow the promise of Jesus-more euphoria you will find to greet
For the opposite of joy-is to think that you are beat
I promise my Maker always-the meaning of the word titled...extol
Wow...angels draw nearer
I kiss her face
And taste a sweet tear
A collection of worth
I see her as nearing perfection-an image of beauty within a mirror
What is the meaning of life?
The secret comes as clean
Look up the term aptly put being...no more contradiction

WRITTEN BY:BRIAN MOILANEN-20024

Down-yes way down

Deal the cards
Yet I must insist please be fair and camouflage who might be owning the ace
Mental efforts concentrate
And a rendering of a fair game I must not trace or abruptly erase
Down-yes way down
I see the hand dealt-this opportunity is a possible mental facade
Do not show a glimpse of emotion-within a deep woods nestled town
Sentiments collaborate yet won't ever show as either confident or even odd
Momentarily I do see red
A loosing hand or will it hold to victory edge?
Call your 6th sense In the ease of use-nothing in which to dread
A glimpse of a smile
A hidden tension in which to cling
Play chance with skill-report to honesty forever and a while
Analyze the faces and see who could be at a bluff
Locate the haphazard chances and put them in an organized file
I hold back a grin and am vigilante to what is not that rough
Play the cards
Play the cards
Or the cards could play you
Internal or is it external parallels
Draw the line as the chosen few
Everyday a new beginning
Albeit in the delivery or even that of a docile safari or zoo
Wise choices
Yet do these choices become profound with luck and chance
My heart rejoices
As my heart strings get plucked and usually dance
Two separate emotions hit me at once and they do collide
Do not overreact as your heart and soul collide
If need be reshuffle what was first hand dealt
Remember we are all in God's country
As a chemistry of faith is quickly felt
No one cut out and no one barred or even kicked out of the scheme
For we are in the holy place-known as the Bible belt
Now every day a new beginning in reverence and strength-enter the dream
Enter a heart with soul
Enter a soul with heart
Shopping for supplies to a thanksgiving of love
Within the grocery store I am ample yet sufficient with this shopping cart
Follow your sentiments
Fulfill with logic and desire
For where there is smoke
You will also find a fire
WRITTEN BY:BRIAN MOILANEN-2020

Driving forgiveness road

Attempting eagerly to track down a hint of genuine clemency
Adding all this up to a sweet kiss of tender mercy
Driving forgiveness road
I know with all attention displaced to only and always give
In due time that I will locate a pristine glorious heaven-the final abode
I too have been wronged and also have wronged many times before
Yet I will reap a bountiful harvest and continue upon this winding road
As a cliché statement-life favors being a dream and certainly not a chore
Is it true or a false pretense-that angels fly high always and in the earth do soar
Today an excellent day to be alive and breathe some unimpaired fresh air it is
My direction takes shapes quickly as I am nearing the ocean and see it's distant shore
A heart that was once burdened Is now relieved and repentance obeys
This game is sometimes although with confusion as I also see uniquely a polar opposite
A newest role of cast members is unending and takes place in theatrical plays
Yesteryear returns in logic and determination that as advised by peers to not ever quit
All walks of life on this planet and attention is given to cut thru the foggy haze
Try to spread words and mention of the steps to forgive and forget
Aim to treat others as you wish to be treated
Foretell and predict from the mind-that their lot in life will improve and they will win the bet
Humbleness is always there-and is not ever in any way conceited
Remember to pray and pray alike to convert the angst into tranquil mind with zero regret
Arm yourself with the cross of Christ and mannerisms that are not defeated
A long road
A long life
A very real dismissal of heartache displaying truth and justice within the code
Turn my back on the struggling state of strife
Mercy says a kind hello
And as for grace it will not ever leave
Remember that with all the interpenetrate and sharing universally we know when to say no
Maybe if my reflections are pure I will gather with what I perceive
Sometimes at the end that somebody somewhere will say to me just go
Yes I firsthand will exclaim and claim that to win is not always the goal
Being engaged in the process is what we will all achieve
Find the depths and degrees of insight
Open the Holy Bible and problems angels on high will intrinsically relieve
Not overnight
Not even necessarily throughout the today
Angels are real
And they esteemed with brilliance make a way
Step out of yourself
And observe what is a justified persona within clarity I must say
A hand that is molding and caressing with inner strength
I hope and pray that I fit the mold of a soft pliable gentle clay

WRITTEN BY:BRIAN MOILANEN-2020

<u>Finding my own failures</u>

Faults

Errors

My own personal efforts that fell apart

Mistakes

The looming and crashing soul thunder

How have I made it even thus far?

My conscience includes me yet also does wonder

Finding my own failures

War stories impose acquisition that of possible plunder

With all of these pristine choices although

Then why do I still find ways to blunder?

Such as the magician that pulls the cute rabbit out of the black hat

Is it real or slight of hand tricks that we all fall under?

Should we evolve or surrender?

I believe that God has put us all together as one and shall asunder

Don't allow your rolling steam train to although come off the track

I aim today to locate my newest home traveling on foot down destitution road

I have my wallet and my cross and also must mention my fully stuffed backpack

Trying and learning new ways to overcome

Is my brain that of I.B.M.?

Yet computers can't superimpose that much and will not know how to hack

Because my part bionic and organic brain today is working

And will I hope not-ever just fail or continue to lack

My mind focuses to yesteryear's bright never ending sun with brilliant shine

Uniquely enough I am fully entwined and mentally speaking as sharp as a tack

I realize that I must forever move onward and am hearing the warbling song of doves

A feeling of sentiment high

Deja-Vu enters the situation and my life is it's record of soundtrack

Ethnicity of all in my red crimson blood

The tabloids we all read are from newspapers and are colored a white and black

The day today is what appears as admiration of silent joy with attached love unique

A drink of red spirited wine

My brain talks to my consoling inner voice and I hear these ambiguous conversations speak

Do you serve God?

Or other unspoken references such as love...how my I sharpen and tweak?

Still working to be the best I can

As I understand all of our days are numbered

And therefore what is my cradle to grave life span?

Must I look for only my grand successes?

Or is that road for me sadly enough just too damn short?

And I look forward as to what brings me down and also what stresses?

Sometimes losers do win

An interesting story of confidence that also blesses

WRITTEN BY:BRIAN MOILANEN-2020

47

Forever fortitude

Seizing eons of time confidently within the forever
Analyzing it all learn to not ever say never
An ongoing battle of good versus evil
Attempting to be kind with my heart-albeit very clever
Forever fortitude
Demonstrating another way with an extra ounce of diligence
A setback indeed with no signals of being rude
There is a bright light at the tunnels end
I keep drawing nearer
As you will agree-all desire to win
Don't give up yet-another plain to see endeavor
The light illuminates the galaxies now
Godly instinct
Yet I will use the cliché statement of...don't have a cow
Choose your side now
The battle is running neck and neck
Play your hand wisely
And when driving on-focus to the 10th degree so as not to have wrecked
Angels of heavenly insight
Guide and preserve us as they protect
Don't discriminate being the same as the Lord
At times including me-lessons of the understanding of true respect
A smiling hug and kiss
Moving each day one step closer to eternal paradise
Abstract methods that obtain us completely to virtues that in time we will all miss
I look into the vastness of the heavens
I see angels in the silvering clouds
Oddly enough I locate a vertical horizon within the television skies
A moderate in color bronze cross gathered within my second sight
Working for the King
Bright sunshine trapped within euphoria and no toil or worry or pain
I see friends that passed
I see family that also has passed
Joy surrounds our every wish and is real and true
Christ is my boss
A path although significant with a narrow way
At times we all become shrouded
Yet follow your own heart strings to hear what I say
We all will stand before Jehovah's throne
And henceforth when you are in-you also will stay

WRITTEN BY:BRIAN MOILANEN-2020

Frequenting with loneliness

All alone
All alone again
A sequence of mental doldrum to that being a temporary struggle
And as for substance today as I see it-difficult to find a win
Frequenting with loneliness
Although many years back I opted to give up the bottle and sinister drugs
All this time I do acknowledge that the inner voice is there
Consolidating with my blessed Maker
A direct life line connection that surfaces as valid and has plentiful care
Out of body experiences
Looking down upon my own beating heart and crazy complex brain
I see uniquely-despite what others might call just a puzzled soul and connective gravity
Sometimes sun-other times a severe pounding of heavy pelting rain
Enough of jeers and peers reminding of my misunderstood yesterday
Where I think without doubt that maybe I am no longer sane
The story I am saying does not aim to cut corners
Just virtues of a tried soul and efforts too not be pushed aside or consoling abrupt pain
Pray for others
Find a soul to hold and squeeze
Elements of this layman locate a supreme tabernacle
Have me awestruck with a pondering newest method to appease
In hindsight more of my life I could rewind only just to play it again
Where I play it much different
So darn much that these peculiar choices although pure-now strangely enough could be sin
Find
Locate
Search the portals of the heart
Just to examine the opening of doors
Without end-without a start
All ages must dream while asleep as the conscience explores
Tired of being lonely
Not alone although that you are
Not the only
The horizons of the planet will guide you and you are now the star

WRITTEN BY: BRIAN MOILANEN-2020

God's heavenly angels

Angels protect

Angels provide

Angels solve problems

Just observe all that they forthright do provide

They can turn a heart–ache into joy

And swinging fists into that of-peace

Sometimes a temporary warzone

We all at times definitely need a spiritual release

Watch the birds in the sky fly-and are they eagles or are they geese?

Finding solace so to say

And my advice is that these souls talk in a subtle tone and comfort the angels above to appease

Action being into that of to pacify and help to remain calm

Let go of panic to seek a redemption of solidarity-in which it does resolve

Speaking to both angels and saints is the untimely subject at hand

I pray for heaven all around too enter my heart and revolve

Common sense liturgy fashions my tenure-draw a line in the sand

Christian rules ensue into what our Dear God does hate

Sin and inequities our Maker put forth in his Testimony to have banned

Finding time to pay and also repent

I give my last ten dollars to a homeless lady

And hope It is in which what I give freely and not ever lent

Not forgetting to always being true

Life can be considered as quite long

Don't dwell on the negative-the substance indicative as being blue

Talking with an earthly angel is my goal

Finding both your heart and soul

Both the good and bad-a way in which to console

Christian rock and roll

I am under the bridge yet playing wisely-only been there twice

As I pray at the toll

Cling and adhere to Christ as King of Kings

Also beit the Lord of Lords

The Prince of peace

The host of hosts

God is everywhere-from the far East and even the Southern coast

Up front

Even down South

Watch what you undeniably occasionally say

Such as being at the theatre

Or like wise-even a weekend matinee

Is life on this planet more complete?

Or are you within fantasy-How about we call it a play

WRITTEN BY:BRIAN MOILANEN-2024

God grant me free love

Unmerited and undeserved kindness
A gift freely given from God's grace above
What happens with relevant testimony from greatness of love
Gifts of free love
Fly with ambitions adored way up high
My soul follows
Hopes to flourish
Please let this understanding find me further-no way to deny
I suppose that contented desire for some leads the way
A procedure of manifested destiny
Do you see the words that I say?
Am I being molded such as the perforated context of clay?
I feel love
I wait on love
Is love the answer?
Is love the forever cure?
Actions and reactions
All succeeding with what is spoken becomes more or less a blur
For its actions are observed by all and like a strong wind it blows
A feeling utmost and uniquely shaken from head to toe
God shares
God cares
Rationalizing my logistics
But typically it just never dares
A give and take
A take and give
The holy wine becomes more than 110% pure and clean
God loves all even his adversaries
Who are without tolerance and at times mean and obscene
Residual inherited kinks within DNA and RNA within accuracy of...
I speculate that this is out of my hands
As I don't know If I fit the mold that is obtained from angels utmost high
Accomplishing this demand of prestige
The understanding of both questions attributed with...wow
Love is a necessity
Love is a must
Love is not tangible
For if it were a machine it could possibly bust
Love so to say is internal
But weather aged or continually wet...it just won't rust
My mind delivers this salutation
And without sin, at times...says...within God we trust
WRITTEN BY:BRIAN MOILANEN-2023

Inspiration(becoming reversed)

You help to keep me alive
Likewise now in a sort-I feel more complete
Rows and channels of partnered romance
As I take slow strides to locate my reserved seat
Love sometimes I cannot deny is very tough to find
Yet when obtained I attempt to cherish and keep
And if this love is lost I am bothered within angst-Reverting my self to rewind
Without her...quickly confusion sets in
My brain wrestles with demons to realize I am freezing and totally confined
Inspiration comes
Inspiration goes
Sustaining within this peculiar creation
Contemplation
Waiting to reclaim my once content heart and tried soul
Although innocent my persona and reputation is lucky to be on parole
Believe you me-at times I pray and hope to never burn in the fiery abyss
Is my hand playing me-or is it the other way around?
Hmm...innocent victim as I frequent mutually with the souls that are lost
As a metaphor did you give away all my love with zero remains to be found?
Hurt within the process
Processing within the hurt
Sad but true
Where is my deep red crimson heart or even that succeeding to an ounce of comfort?
Inspirational joy
It will locate me again
A crashing of the tide the dark angry waves pull me nearly in
This sea of madness is portrayed as hellish and seems as if sin
Inspiration forthright comes and also goes
On this abacus I count both my wins and losses
Along with it's countless friends and even undermined by foes
Some answers
Other days you will hear the screams of anger supplied with the no's
Doing my damnest to locate a fit
But I stand tall armed with obscurity and none the less-still see red
I smoke a cigarette and rely only on the means too not quit
Balancing both polar opposites-one being zest and the other being dread
Remember these words that allure and yet also entice
My understanding is trivial
And today I see all in a maze that are in the shadows and run like loose mice

WRITTEN BY:BRIAN MMOILANEN-2020

Intimate with your soul

Just where to start?
Or in layman's terms specifically
When is the right place or time to begin?
As for me my soul gets ultimately tried
Yet I am human and I cannot just give way to sin
But sin and tribulation is within the midst
And my own faltering methods locate a back door
A measure although inevitable
For sometimes life is a bombastic circumstance and a perpetuated chore
I am drawing nearer to my conscience and heart
Furthermore I must add sometimes l am high and other times low
Emotions of impedance are located as contrary
And my forbearance is there which is beginning to grow
I must not self destruct and go into sabotage
I must be stealth like and as a boxer twist and dodge
For sometimes my feelings are vaguely understood as looking at a mirage
Make sure uniquely in spite to serve God
He will guide and ordain and supply with what you need
Even though perfection or discretion apparently appears as odd
Plant the seeds of love
And culture them in the early spring and within the grass and sod
Christ has love and power that just won't end
Repair the areas of frailty that are put on occasionally-feelings dispose
And they also begin or end within a gesture-watch them bend
Take time if willing to extol or at a minimum to pray for your your foes
Time is short
And eventually someday your days will close
Like a book
But when is the exact end-that much nobody knows
Sometimes we just won't agree
A situation that I just cannot oppose
Nobody is perfect
And our track records emulate what stops and also what grows
Spirits say hello
Angels let us find a clean path
Take a moment to reflect
And cleanse your being within a tumultuous bath
A little noisy
A little loud
Can you hear Christ from afar?
Just to balance both the humble along with the proud

WRITTEN BY:BRIAN MOILANEN-2022

Jumping to conclusions

Judging

Is often times-not legitimate or right

A form of jumping to conclusions

Mixed feelings-a peaceful man I am yet now want to fight

Unfair methods cause confusion and chaos even down to my very sight

Outdoors the wind denies as only downward plummets this once sailing kite

I too have judged yet aim to modify these ways

Doing charades and miming to act within local traveling concerts and also plays

Intrusion

Seclusion

Making my life that of an institution

Making hallucinated fact out of fiction

This also understood as a delusion

Form your own conclusion

Combined these separate elements

This the mainstay that being the word fusion

Yet remember that when you judge

You will also be judged '

And at whatever you measure

Likewise you will also be measured

Hypocrites claim to right-yet more times than most are wrong

And this poem that I write I bet you could also edit or alter

Brain activity muses to form an anchored yet also subjective song

Treat your neighbor as yourself and make efforts not to falter

And when in heaven remember that there is no time-infinity shall be forever and is a beautiful strong

We on the earth have all entertained angels without knowledge of

This in itself is euphoria triumphant

As in the darkest of days we will hear the joy of the warbling dove

Take time to reflect

And at this added notion-do you ponder to think that this biblical utterance could just be a hint

A hint for love

A time for peace

Save a soul Bye God

Can"t you find what is innocent and freed as an angelic release

Written by:Brian Moilanen 2020

Keeping concurrent with balance

Life at times can throw a lot our way
Do you know what I mean-furthermore-do you know what I say?
A changing of the rushing tide
Within nostalgia-as if living again-and at the Y-2K?
A day that is chilly and distraught but I will help you see It thru
Keeps me level-headed and not trafficking within an exotic human zoo
Fears come and they go
Paranoia Is caused by an innocent heart yet is acting as in trouble
Yet you are the holding the deflating pin
And it is I that holds the gigantic large bubble
It is uniquely an angelic answer I suppose because a clean conscious…
Is obtained by being true to the self
And forthright with your spouse and neighbor
I have to sweeten the pot-
An absolution that is both tried and true
Take care of yourself and not forget to mention-also your health
How many more tomorrows
Quite animatedly-remaining upon your shelf?
Love is passive
True-it both comes and goes
Blending in I hope
And caste within both my friends and also my foes
Yet keep in check that when confronted with animosity and hate
It is none the less in the cards-at times-and derives from fate
Showing up early is on time
And showing up on time is late
Play your cards with good ability
And be careful too not let others forcibly push their weight
Use it to motivate-not to deteriorate
A lesson learned by all eventually
Stick around-at times patience is a virtue
Each day henceforth fashions as adequate
When bored silly-take time to both pray and if need be-comfortably sit
Keeping concurrent with balance
A systemic energy to help with deadlines and goals
The Holy Word now being held by sinners and saints
As we all know Christ had an undying passion for all to be free
From both the North and South Poll
A parent's dream someday will find accord with me to
I do not have children or offspring
Too much free time makes me ask what next to do
Learn as mentioned to repent
And if someone disagrees-tell them to get bent
The effectual fervent prayer avails man very much
This being a treat for me and you
And apparently you are possibly an earth angel-with a sweet-and-soft touch

WRITTEN BY:BRIAN MOILANEN-2024

Last summer's romance

Love at first sight
No time to waste
Such as frosting on a cake
That illustrates in good fashion and even better taste
A sweet and white element of picture perfect
Fashion with a lively paste
Last summers romance
How fast love left me down
My clothes are unusually dirty
And now it appears all I wear is a frown
Her subtle with glowing smile
To be with Rozanne I would walk the length of this earth
Let alone another acre or mile
She has a beautiful smile and is attractive as can be
I have waited my whole life ...which is a long while
Eons of time and space yet no true way to keep tab
I miss her so much
As I pick up the phone and alarmingly decide to dial
She is poised with the free gesture of true love and what a touch
Love although never truly dies
Do you agree?
And henceforth just what are your replies?
The test of time
We all know occasionally this can put us thru the times that try
I am certain my love that you agree
And together we will comply
You are in my mind and heart and don't forget to mention also my soul
Life can be seen and observed as sort of a game
The dice are in my hands as I take my turn to give the their role
There is infinity within every moment
The good Lord has put this belief in my psyche
So much time yet with that said I ask for forgiveness and also repent
Where are you now
I plead and cry for your return
As someday I know and attain to make a vow
You have beauty
You are sweet
You are clever
And you shape me to be complete
I woke up this morning to my phone on beeping
It is you
As meloncholy hits me and I am torn between smiling and weeping
You are back in my life
I love you and this much goes without even saying
I do my homework
And continue to keep all in mind as I keep on praying
Heaven will be our next home
Yes that much is true
Yet sometimes all I need is you
I love you
Forever and forever
Until death do us part
You are im my soul and mind
Also within my body and pumping heart

WRITTEN BY:BRIAN MOILANEN-2022

LOVE ALWAYS FINDS A WAY

Okay

Okay

I am having some heavy thoughts today

It appears that a disparage of hate and animosity are finding me

I do not know what to do to solve this diabolical servitude

I aim to be polite and attentive to all

Yet am kind of strung out-forgive me if I seem rude

My attitude seems corrupt-sheer confusion takes it toll and let alone a fall

Love always finds a way

Will it shine on me now and not continue to haphazard as huge and become small

We all for the most part are I imagine good

Yet I say do what you must

And pay attention to what you should

What involves me to drive to succeed

The same as you

These colors are bright

And do not suffice as to being overtly worn out and are actually brand new

Recall through your mental images of both the good and the bad

Are these emotional wavelengths withstood and understood as only a few

Is this security measure for those deemed fit and iron clad?

Think it over

Respond to the soul

A life well lived

In solemn voice should not feel as if on parole

Live live free

Obtain your role

Inner clocks

Who did the winding and set me in play

Do you know what I mean

Do you hear the words that I say

Middle ground seeks to strive

It also seeks to locate a win and any included absolution

Content

Repent

Do not become although hell bent

Heaven sent

A seasons time for the Saviour-if up to speed observe Lent

Angelic twist

Represents this surreal gist

If possible walk away from a fight

To avoid an enemies fist

Love thy neighbor as thyself

A child's dream

A smiling and giving chilly weathered Christmas elf

Martyr

To die for

Testing faith exclusively with tremendous obstacle

Or am I holding the hand of misfortune?

My enemy aims too pull the wool over my eyes-yet just another battle

Stymied with a situation that is far from acquiring a grin

For this matter of difficulty is heard by the the crowd and many do tattle

Just how to always be on the side of peace?

Or is it the other way around?

Hope is destined as a zeal of nu-found effort needing a release

Clinging to sanity and not following the cards of a clown

Trapped within time and space

Battling again yet forward motion is the system key and is far from wavy shore

A component of perfection-this unprecedented agenda I can't deny

The host of poverty finds today a free meal titled destitution

Mental mind games consist of verbal pollution

Yet what to do specifically for an absolute restitution?

I have I been thrown into psyche wards and likewise institutions

Yet I don't give in

Fighting to win

Avoiding the crowd that attracts a crowd

And further more doing pretty good to turn from sin

Cardinal sin that is overtly loud yet not proud

This fight I can't lose so therefore I will substantiate to a knockout of a win

Allegations of treating and serving the King with a mindful of reply

Answers to my questions as mentioned a moment ago

All I then need to do Is just try

God shall wipe away the tears and contort the grimace or even the whimsical sigh

For every emotion I have and that which is obtained by circumstance

Repent

Give my life to convert to a save

Knocking on heaven's door

Yet still footsteps from my shallow grave

Why all of the lack of balance in this world?

Find the dusty road and if opted beit then continue to pave

If need be I will give my life

And have suffered immensely for justice sake

Like that of skipping stones on a frigid iced lake

Memory strain

Absurd yet astonishing painful memories
Painful recollections of my past attempt to penetrate and invade
Playing cards dealt from the bottom of a stacked deck
Oddly this hand is losing despite this ace or spade
Heavenly skies focused upon me portrayed as maize blue or even green jade
The Holy Bible uniquely keeps me alive
Oceans shadowed by lakes, rivers, and seas at large
Within these abodes of infinity and dwelling I do dive
I am quite alone with sentiments that as decayed fruit becoming rancid
Where what was once sweet no longer does thrive
Hatred fuels this intense rapid fire
Animosity is difficult to hold back
I realize these head trips are due to being ostracized
Please believe me as I inspire to pick up any slack
Why oh why
I repeat in my mind
I aim to succeed but you make me miserable with malice and hate
I can't win
And although confused I am not late
It looks like free will has lost and I become the subject of hate
You can fool all of the people some of the time
And some of the people all the time
I drink this beverage construed with both lemon and lime
I must make this beating heart as tarnished no longer
I am becoming fast and feeling even stronger
The psyche of my very soul
Entertains the angels that have not given up on me
They open my ears and allow me to vividly see
Feelings and emotions perplex as one
God above please forgive
Deciphering between work and fun
Soften the heart and spirit and spirit to
A rendition of decency located me just now
And love is without color but its actions are seen as they grew
Heal
Take a moment to understand and reveal
Love entwines is very evident and forthright real

WRITTEN BY:BRIAN MOILANEN-2022

Mind games

Games are sometimes caused within having a cruel heart
An honest soul weighs in on the scrutiny
Sometimes although this is caused by having a broken brain
You do see the light again and again
Yet at times I do feel as if in an undeniable mental pain
Back off
As I will make my final stand
Do you see and feel these logistics of overall concern?
Do your homework
As both the you and I shall continue to succeed and at the same time will learn
Words can boost
Or they can break
Follow the proper route
To avoid being another burning soul within a perdition being a fiery lake
Learn and adjust the way that ultimately you do live
Sometimes obviously we all do take
And at other times-some just give and give
And will also mention to you that this world is not truly always fair
Are you content?
Or quite obviously we all do at times do take
And at other times the ingredients of construe-they leek like a sieve
If so inspired pick up the Good Book
If you gather-I should say to you the Holy Bible
If you have never read any of it before
Open it up to escape from the doldrums of your complicated life
And locate a content heart that surfaces away from being a never-ending chore
Going back to the beginning-so be it-the very start
Mind games-why so much cruelty within this planet earth
Why is there so many crazy ways that equate to being abrupt
At times as mentioned-it occasionally does not make sense
My heart stays concurrent with the current days and times
But I do see that none the less as lacking-and also apparently very dense
Blessed if you will
Blessed if you won't
Blessed if you do
Blessed if you don't
Maintain this solace and strength with your steadfast character
Make up your mind and once and for all
Sometimes fashioning as cures for everyone upon this planet earth
Bye the way-is it where we will shall all end?
Or let alone is it the fundamentals of where we begin-call it a precious birth?
Remember to be kind
Karma is beyond true
You Do I suspect are adjusted on the right path
Perdition or paradise to follow?
Don't give up-take my hand-I will help you see it thru

WRITTEN BY:BRIAN MOILANEN-2024

Missing you now and forever

Living without you is quite an irreversible endeavor
Am I speculating within the laws of nature and of truth?
Are these words simple but remotely clever?
Missing you now and forever
Time as of yet is not removing this hurt and healing this wound
Yet I still await
Does this sound as being achievable?
And furthermore speaking within logistics is this opportune?
Pictures of you
Clutter my bedroom and floor
Sailing away are sweet memories
A sea among all the distance and no near-bye shore
Where furthermore does time go when it is used up?
I walk these streets endlessly
And gather pocket change from strangers into a beggars hand and coffee cup
Where are you now I will and must imply?
A system of events that continually change
Which opposes the need of courage to let alone even try
Yet I am firm that I will be with you again
You look at me with prying and avenging eyes
Did I turn from the Holy Bible and its precept?
Did I do wrong and furthermore did I sin?
A mind full of memory and it is well kept
Inner clocks
Who did the winding
Inner clocks
Interest we are finding
I love you
Spoken from soft subtle voice
You love me
Forever to rejoice
Do you remember who I am?
Are you possibly in a whirlwind of dismay?
Human beings take shape within our Dear Lord and makers hand
May we say that we are human clay?
So many questions
Have I lost temporarily my way?
No just answers come to mind as of yet
The cards may be stacked against me
But raise the ante for I will win this bet?
All I want to know is did you love me as I am
Take me as you see me
Life is a continuation of tests
And onward for these tests I do readily cram
Sometimes I feel as an innocent and earnest policeman
So many friends and wondering how to sustain my past arrests?
Live the law
And furthermore
Uphold those fondly innocent
Yet knowing sometimes we all do fail
Therefore I put my praying into action and also do repent
So much time now all alone
My story is over and also spent

WRITTEN BY:BRIAN MOILANEN-2022

Mystified by being molded

Words can boost

Words can break

Tame complex situations that deflect into inner rage

This actually defies as in the garden of Eden-portrayed as a cunning snake

A crafty brilliant being that bolsters as evil and you attain more as you flip the Bible's page

Cryptic writings and differing bibles on this marbled mantle

Yet these efforts of consoling soothe my angel mind and henceforth also my brain

My soul was once hungry yet now currently is full

Fire up the corvette

That serves as a drive to win

Don't attest to being chagrin

And henceforth paint over with crosses the undeniable stain

The gasoline burns not only fuel

It also umbrellas rain and seals away your pain

Throw away the past sins with fervent fire

Inspire

Hire

Don't toil upon needless energy

As in heaven foremost-you will not ever even tire

If you aren't a believer

Then how did we come about this now known angelic empire?

Saving the lost

Saving others that in the garbage can were tossed

Mystified

Hard to understand

Difficult to grasp and hold

Pulling straws and drawing cards

That give warmth in the frigid December cold

Rules

Decrees

I pray to my higher power upon these bowed knees

A method of qualified deliverance

Which at least nearing my sanity's edge begins to appease

Contentment rallies

And if have wronged you an answer comes that of...please?

Forgiveness doesn't have any financial cost

Counting once again both my wins and losses very avidly

I contain and revert to Holy word

Which to the spiritual being is done with logic easily

I beg for other's retribution

And am sure that you can worldwide hear this plea

WRITTEN BY:BRIAN MOILANEN

77

No decisions today

Optimism begins to fade and slowly dies
Going to obtain never the less a pure scarlet heart both clean and absolute
Although my conscious of virtue locates quickly conflict that forever tries
A hate that never subsides
Only and now forever I must be true to spirituality and allow love that uniquely implies
Love
Pray for an answer
Subside the mentality of feeling as angry again
Once again love ultimately will win
Turn the absurd situations backward-detour form wrath to turn henceforth from sin
Dreams
Screams
Trust in this source of judgment and doctrine
A hello salutation pervades as we envelope both shining sun and moonlight beams
A wispy letter from a loved one year's ago echoes in my heart and total ego
Yet I must not be with a big ego as this edges out my very God
Remember that being with love and water and sun a dark soul begins to grow
Retain the past in the brain if need be
A recollection of yesteryear views fireflies as a dark night gives that truly do glow
No decisions today
Tomorrow the day of redemption
With probability of profusion of angels
We all will be standing before the King in judgment-no exception
Pray for forgiveness
Plead your case and change any evil thought that you may have had
For without good this planet of planets would die
Remember this cliché statement...it all uniquely is not bad
Repent
Ask others to do the same
Without condolence although do not judge
And as this unique method might someday modify in token...it's all the same
Some only pray-others just seem to sin
Remember the elderly
And adversely also from the Wizard of Oz...the mechanical man made of tin
Do not pop the child's bubble
And disregard the need for now at least-the sharp and altering pin

WRITTEN BY:BRIAN MOILANEN-2020

NOISE

A hear a noise that is far beyond tumultuous
And in essence-beyond really loud
Trapped between two separate distinctions
This being bright sun within a dark cloud
The ambience of weather never does discriminate
As it shakes up weather wisely I pray and have bowed
The crackling of thunder continues to apparently rage
I read a Holy Bible as the angels watch on high
Quite a surreal –so to say; it is time to turn one more page
Shot heard round the world
A spark ignites into the heavens
Uniquely I only although with these four cards
The tally of these cards being that of only number sevens
An extension of sound
Noise
That beats like a drum inside this very brain
The skies silver, grey, and nearly black
The pouring rain paints a picture but is oddly that of a stain
Watch the white shaded lightning as it does crack
People do talk
Some others just scream and shout
Distant decibels find me as though that they do stalk
A soft cry from a toddler that today does often times pout
The still calmness before the raging storm
A balancing act of the intricate senses
Even the angels of Jehovah God are tried very untimely to the norm
Make the grade and shine your light to find a method that in which does conform
Occasionally in my head I hear words that are quite brash
Do your homework as honest as possible-make effort to never properly inform
Occasionally in my head I hear words that are expelled as brash
My vocation is honest-I feel as if at times like a Catholic Priest
We are all within a test-yes a test-that is to say the least
As of now the heavens up above strangely just don't storm
Save a soul from hellfire-with indescribable pain-catered from an evil beast
Where is it that you will make your view of this stand?
Vigilante colleagues from a type of superior interest
Forgiveness-yet on the other hand
Sometimes you need to fall within the right time-just always give your best
An honest and complete soul
Will always get their sleep-call it that of rest
Noise
We are nearing the Armageddon
Scholars and Bible backers also do agree
This world when armed with love
Will always outshine what is evil
A genius of even philosophy and religion itself-my conscience does see
The world that we live always does change
And-as you know-change is good
Pick your Lord wisely-the quality of does rearrange

WRITTEN BY:BRIAN MOILANEN-2024

Now that you are gone

Now that you are gone
Cleanly divided within my soul cut smack dab in the middle
I would give a billion dollars just to see you smile once again
Yet apparently notice that just won't do my dream becomes small and little
But dreaming is good and never has been noticed or observed as any sin
The Pied Piper won't lead my life with or without a fiddle
I am not striving for a tie only to obtain a legitimate win
Although having some difficulty understanding that God does free the innocent
A preponderance of intrigued truth maybe this I suspect is that of an acquittal
Some say life is a constant effort of good versus bad
Make friends with those that play their cards close to the chest
Becoming awestruck this neighbors with going mad
All the madness with commotion I suppose that angels will take time to vest
Is this a mid life crisis because I feel rather blue and apparently sad
What causes feelings, frets, and emotions?
The heart sees that this question causes me to feel quite adrift and very high
For occasionally I get lost and am alone and trapped in this deep blue ocean
Do you think of me much?
Glowing with sentiment I am still in tune
Yet with you here no longer I desperately do I drive endlessly for this magic touch
The stage you have set without desire am I a buffoon?
Love
The scales of justice tip and turn
Joy
Busting lawbreakers in this world is now my concern
I truly wish that you were here
Honest effort
I remain and stand as a lover and also a peer
It is apparent that your belief in a higher power is strong and vast
While remaining sincere
Cast out those demons and whatever that does ail
Obstinate and recreate I don't allow for this darned fear
And must I add don't intend to fail
The physical sense is free yet as for the brain and mind it sometimes feels as if in jail
Life plays its cards with me and you
For we are all in a play and surrounded by a stage
Domesticated humans earn the heavenly pledge
And are not contained within imprisonment or even a cage
Some concur to put a title of self righteousness on the awaiting party
Yet aim to not label or give a believed belief of an individual
For what counts to me is a effort applied to amount towards forming a win
Winning of a good heart
Winning of a tried soul
Most pass the test
And it is apparent that they took time to invest
Now that you are gone'
You took a part of me with you
Sadly as just mentioned-you took a part of me

WRITTEN BY:BRIAN MOILANEN

Of which to ponder

Homelessness
Out on the street
A situation that definitely tries the whole psyche
As the soul follows and dislodged becomes mayhem and also defeat
Yet you are the lock and your personal savior is the turning key
Weathered and withered yes-yet please don't say the word beat
Bottom of the barrel
How to avoid this anger within-my senses follow being very heated
Fingers pointed at me from the uncaring individuals
For their hearts are unjust and also deliberately conceited
A game of mouse chasing cheese at times
All have done what is necessary and also replied with having competed
A grim situation
Particularly solemn and corrupt
I aim although not to bring you down
And not enter in the scales weighing in at quite abrupt
Your pockets may not even have that of a buck or two
Your religion in the stratosphere of goodness uniquely although isn't ever bankrupt
A walk thru the park is listless and strange resembling a human zoo
Inspired a bit with the heavenly skies more or less now
Which is that of a color resembling baby blue
More to add-It's hard to detect whether these shades although institute the hue
If I were a human robot-or even an android
Do I need fixing-and if so, would you turn my mechanical operating screw?
Back on the street
Back to the autumn chill
A closure I none the less seek
I will climb in progress this mountain of never-ending hill
My motors possibly need turning
I must locate and adjust this out of balance mechanical body
Survival of the fittest-my intestines are churning
Pain in this body is prevalent
A pain ever-wrenching keeps me on course-and is warm and almost burning
I never ever give up interestingly enough
Frugal consistency-by nature is not timid and obtains learning
Searching for food to eat
Searching henceforth for water to drink
Will I hunger again?
Diplomatic justice-I pull the short straw and am on the brink
Follow your instincts of candid chemistry of lasting until the end of time
I cry hard for a first time intelligence-my emotions heavy and at oceans edge do sink

WRITTEN BY:BRIAN MOILANEN-2020

One day nearer to paradise

I play my cards close to the chest
My boundaries are marked and I attest to stand firm
Time to invest with strong stamina to confess
Stand my ground
Make effort not to get coerced and pushed around
Life is a game
Searching for important clues within the lost and found
This life challenge sometimes has many restraints
A debacle of legitimate substance
One mans health cures and has found a way yet one dies and awkwardly faints
A picture of glamour and virtues added within to create a solution
The paintbrush is resilient-watch what it uniquely paints
In this Mother earth most see it as a battle ground of bad and good
Bad news travels often quicker although than the good
Completely trivial
And known by most as what is truly misunderstood
I have spoken to holy angels
I pray within realms of spirituality
When more persons are saved-gifts come like no other
For when you add it all up
It is a virtue of both brothers and sisters
Drink the blood of Christ in the challis
Jesus paid the price for all implying the substance of sinners and saints
Furthering into this testimony saints and sinners
Embellishing for the poor
Good choices don't perish-they tend to consummate
A good life I speculate is both a give and take
A give and share
A live and learn
I too have been half tempted
Yet my engine is idling which allows it to churn
The tables do turn
If you are right within a situation-the opposition lights their own fire
As onlookers watch what evils they promoted to burn
Pray
Become bestowed that it is what you do
And also with you say
Life can be incredibly tough
But if you rely on your laurels you will locate what Is true
As is with a detective
And consecrating evidence as a true deed
And the intent of what assembles any motive
Someday we will all be at the gates of heaven-yes someday
'That is when the grade will be made
This is reality my friend and not a play
WRITTEN BY:BRIAN MOILANEN-2023

One world to live?

What is your belief on the understanding of other planets having living life?
Draw the understandings of considerably belief
Unimportant analogy of direction is it me with the strife?
One world to live
Is there one or more planets that we would and should have come to light?
Enough darkness to compose a UFO possibly this very night
As we know although that two wrongs do not constitute a right
Are there tens of thousands that envelope this critical 6th sense of sight
True this is the only location with life abroad and vibrant with hope that we know
The candle burns ever so dimly on fire to admire
And as for now I do see plain as day-flashing space oddities that in the heavens do glow
It would be selfish to act in methods of speculating that we are all alone-what remains to desire
If I am wrong let me hear the inner drive to detour and avoid this detrimental woe
How to move although when I have in angst a barren and flat tire?
Religion and Christianity may take the upper hand
Yet how just to abandon my own personal belief when roasting marsh-mellows at the camp fire?
Yet what about astrology and science endeavor-which study is true and in command?
Other planets
Other solar systems
Other lands and worlds
Stack up the age long processes of study and speculation
Not everything is fact or either fiction
A gray area that is surreal and entertains the curious within all and in particular this creation
Inner clocks
Interest we are holding and finding
Where comes the drive to strive when everything else proves to be coming short
Inner clocks-play the tape though and if need be do the rewinding
Glue the edges down
As they in time only resurface for only an ample binding
I know that we are not in an alien ant farm
Be careful what you wish for
As the direct component of belief is belief-shining with illustrious mention or charm
Confusion transfusion
Audible volumes within this crisis of text albeit telepathy
Crystal ball and the like-a total discourse of illusion?
Hallucination or is it angels on high that stare back in truth-Evangelical road-do you agree?
Palm reading
Fiction or fact
Tarot cards
Black magic and white magic also are observed
Delusion propels us with turmoil
An interest for knowledge and love is now all that is served

WRITTEN BY:BRIAN MOILANEN-2020

Perceptions

What one believes as true
Another may believe it is false
Similar to a delusion-is it indicative that your heart is true?
Just with the reading of the jugular vein-Is it accurate I would assume that you have a pulse?
Yet speaking with objectivity in mind
Isn't it true that paranoia has different aspects to it...
Irrational fears that bounce back again and again?
Innocence speaks frantically-of just why and when?
The human mind
So complex and intricate it is a scientific and spiritual journey indeed
Take heed to what I speak and say
The Holy bible talks and perceptions of and for it does also read
Idiosyncratic beliefs attached to impressions
That are firmly maintained in spite of what is generally accepted to it's outcome
Ignorance sometimes
The calloused and frail bum never stops his or her survival test
Yet without shelters and churches maintained as their lodge
Just how are they able to get a night of rest
Burnt out and tiring-loitering tickets force them out of dodge
It's a bird
Others claim it's a plane
A flying saucer-I refer to the mundane
How to save?
And therefore-maybe I should focus on myself
Taken for granted the mainstay of public becomes
As for me though I aim not to thirst as I rummage the drinks upon the market shelf
See what this all leads to...
Rates of turmoil seem to raise the roof
And also the bar
My thoughts and behaviors fail-I have become aloof

WRITTEN BY:BRIAN MOILANEN-2020

Pictures of you

Pictures of you
A facade of unique chemistry
Testimony allocates truth asking to be set free
Sometimes I notice only a middle road turmoil
Yet none the less I play it straight-for this is me
Where have all of the yesterdays gone?
Pieces to a perplexing puzzle
Yet I am working to solve with a heart of a stance that is honest
I move also cautiously with that of a pawn
Endless hours where a madness invades as I slowly clench this tightening fist
Sunlight enters converting dusk into a pristine beautiful sunny dawn
Who is who?
...and for that matter just what is what?
Do I even have a clue?
I feel and hear a restless vessel within my pitted gut
Angel soul
Find yourself
Then you will find me
An angel within us all
That is tame and always hopes that you will agree
No strings attached
A head full of drama and although innocent-will you please listen to my plea?
Every breath Is one breath closer to heaven
And also innocence sees that another baby is born
A haphazard glance at my watch indicates that it is seven to eleven
Although at times I am truly weak
I know and accept that absolution will find a new home
As I will be back with greater fortitude to both seek and tweak
Inquiring in modest fashion with angels to forgive and freely roam
Every picture that is taken reflects an image of a particular time
A particular place
A particular sentiment
Grinding out any hatred to see light that will shine
Spirits of sacred souls
A sun that always is prevalent and noticed from both the north and south poles
Time to change
A change in time
For I am your lover with a musical understanding
And you are the verse and also the angelic rhyme
Yes life and love can be tough at times-Your heart strings are commanding

WRITTEN BY:BRIAN MOILANEN-2020

Please forgive me

Obviously I am the same as you
Parts of me are laden with mistakes
I without any doubt see occasionally holy angels
Yet as for you it appears that you see only mythological evil and eerie snakes
At times I was seen with wide open eyes
Yet often times now these eyes do and will close
Giving valor freely to my close friends
And antidotes of medicine to my ever present foes
Please forgive me
Marching forward
Please forgive me
While stepping momentarily backward
If time grows knowledge-am I therefore now wise?
Recalculating this game plan
With confidence I climb-a method that at the spur of the moment I revise
Another slammed door-tail between my legs
Christ payed the price of mankind's sins forever
Hung to dry on a cross with its agonizing bloody pegs
If you do not believe this
Your conscience someday only begs
These unfailing eyes
And angels sweet kiss and dreams for this measure will abound
A sweet yet short whisper from an angel
Golden glowing halos of a pearl white and golden bronze
There is no way to measure as I would understand it...perfection
A calculated game of power versus pawns
Does this make sense?
The kids in summer gather sunlight and sit in their lawns
Forgive your neighbor
Your neighbor I pray forgives you
Family and friends
To name all or even just a few
Make the logical choice
And do what you must-do what you need to do
More signs of divinity
Saintly and moving onward
For a small percent some were blind-but now ultimately see
Am I a professor of common logic?
And even if we don't see eye to eye-somewhat will you agree?
A medicine that actually helps-do you hear my undying and unwavering plea
Praying
Absolution
Kind deeds
An angel cries as an angel pleas
A plea to terminate those that have an evil way
Emotions run
As emotion also does play
A color or tint that has run smudged and is the color of grey
Black and white
That has been formed and is if clay

WRITTEN BY:BRIAN MOILANEN 2022

95

Seeds of an empty and vacant heart

Planting and cultivation
Seeds of an empty and vacant heart
So to say a million miles from the end
Moreover eons from the beginning that is also defined as the start
All I cling to is pure sentiment as I devise a method developing this change of mend
It is unprecedented that obviously certain times were sweet and others tart
I take a moment to reflect even deeper as angels and Jehovah have miracles to send
The ball of wax unravels I realize yet it won't come apart
I check my mailbox daily for my God Letter- I until further notice shall attend
Some people without innuendo I must add only straighten and correct
And others with added mischief and vile ways mangle and bend
Time can take it's toll
Live as you survive to track down a smile or two
The fireplace fires up for nights on end yet has no wood or oddly enough even coal
Finding and counseling souls that appear dispirited yet light the way for the hungry few
Today a day unique the bridge not burnt as I pay the 10 cent toll
Lean towards what drives you
The chemistry is partial which inclines too some as intuition
Conscious understanding takes a back seat to a learned instinct
Can't you see
Won't you hear
The magnificence of cut red roses
Along with this story may bring a crystal tear
I know that you have it hard
Yet I know that the fear of Godly good will make salvation utmost clear
Choose and pick your battles with added wisdom
Make friends with the Lord
A fight my friend that you will win
Yet no there is no bloodshed despite the last angel left is clinging to his sword
I realize that at frequent times depression may hit
Yet like wise the tables in which this applies may turn
As you know even our Savior's homework was the Holy Bible kit
Teaching doctrines and covenants as those amassed did learn
Sometimes bleak
Other days great
Sometimes It's difficult to find even words itself that speak
I believe that we create our own fate
The prosperous fruits sustain and the others unfortunately just wreak

WRITTEN BY:BRIAN MOILANEN-2020

Standing high and mighty

Petrified within angst we hear the people scream
Henceforth others begin to blatantly yell
Another fortunate soul is freed with the cross of Christ
The story narrated by the holy angel reveals good versus evil so much to tell
Be bold and learn to give respect
Live free and don't ever neglect
This salvation happens haphazardly and pays virtue to justice
A train that stays on the tracks and that has not wrecked
Backbone
For most grows stronger through progress of time
If you can't fall in love
Find that venting frustration comes with an uphill climb
Emotions
Feelings
Response to whatever the sentiment or situation brings
Where is the guarantees of youth and adult and everything in between
A lifetime of living as we all acquire purpose and testament that clings
Heart of a champion
Not forgetting to mention failures which we all can attest to
Sometimes and rarely winners do quit
Yet beat the odds and watch the world of yours take shape-adhesive is the glue
Recession hits us all-live concurrent with good to shun from the abyss or pit
Follow rules of your own pumping heart and blood in veins
You at the given time hold the power so don't...
Ever let loose this undying power attributed with gifts and clouds with
You can't bring me down
It takes a nation of millions too hold me back
From a thriving metropolis to a small little town
I am not a hunter or the prey-I'm a strong man not of either opposition with minimal lack
Some give in
Some give out
Some don't try at all
And others just pout
In time what usually occurs is manifestation
And it is anchored with songs of whispers all the way too a shout
Pay attention to your elders
Give respect to all
Pray for those innocent who serve time
As the hands of justice will sway and Karma will find us now without a fall
Love
Not so easy to achieve
Yet once you obtain it
Grasp and hold and cling-proclaiming the status of believe
BRIAN MOILANEN-2020

Taught how to cry

The first time I ever cried
A valuable lesson in these crystal tears running down my face
Yet just exactly how much was comprehended as the indecisive had not denied
Not quite sure
Wet eyes will not ever suit me-I gather and did confide
Stay buckled in this luxury of what we all will endure
Attempting to be positive
I guess that I do not know and also comply with I am not sure
Some are negative
Aggravation sees the route of complex emotion
A landslide of feelings meeting sentiment
A river or some body of feeling and poise-tears do not contain this lamented ocean
A passing of family member or even a dear friend
How much is relieved by the simplicity to just weep
I have a stance to anchor in the pit of uncertainty and see an end
Misty eyed
I pray for all angels to send light via Jesus calling
The engine is running
Yet appears to also be stalling
Taught how to cry
Life a perception of perception itself
I stare back at the mirror
And wonder how much more time looks back upon this marbled shelf?
Centuries or decades or even years with attached days
Cutting through this mustard and ordained with light
Yet trickled in the picture is also an angry haze
A vehement time
A moment to solemnly reflect
Changing my cards if able-trading these cards at the poker table
Reshuffle the cards and refrain if need be to ultimately inspect
Little ones and kids
Kids and little ones
You will cry
And maybe quite a bit
Understand these words as impact of being true
Yet a great tiding steps in
And maybe it is just me that does not know what to do
Time on your side
Let this ramification of thought make you being that of brand new
Find a soulmate
Call it your partner or other half
Remember to follow the lead of good loving parents
As the kids grow up quickly and will grow tall as a giraffe

WRITTEN BY:BRIAN MOILANEN-2020

The collapse of courage

Such as a decaying bridge
The collapse of courage
I walk ever so steadfast along the mountain nearing the hilly ridge
I aim to not ever give up
Yet a paradox of negative emotion begins to set in
I won't give up in spite of
Yet it can be vitally intrusive and the passing of it is an allotment that is chagrin
Who holds the needle?
And with that said just who is holding the puncturing pin?
Sentimental knowledge seems so precise yet varies in its depth and feeling
Think before you speak
As the gambler collects and also is now dealing
Repair the bridge and shoot to not burn it although your feelings are cantankerous
Divisive and looking to argue is just a pretense now
So much has been worked for and these days I will definitely miss
Two separate emotions deluge in my mind all at once
Remember we live by how we play-goodness and salvation pull this soul from the abyss
And my folks did not make an idiot or even a dunce
Stay strong
Live by if possible the golden rule
A land with a populace of billions
Greed does not contend
As a common goal to achieve in ultimate display
Christ is the answer for all
And agony subsides this very day
Try something new
Although I am not a king I desire to be my best
This short refection of thought is best if not censored
The skies are currently now pouring rain and my palms are moist and wet
Such as a fish chasing the bait the probability is allured
If I were you I would not be comfortable just to get what I get
Call out now in the name of God to stop all wars
Repair the burnt bridges and pray for peace
Jesus is coming soon for the 2nd time
Components of virtue liven and extenuate for this soul and it's release
Change your ways
That goes for me to
The religion of religion and feeling of is out of this world
And it is a one size fits all shoe
W.W.J.D.
What would Jesus do
Houses of the holy
A breath of fresh air-not a human zoo

WRITTEN BY:BRIAN MOILANEN-2020

The immortal portal

Take heed
This life is substantially just a glimpse of beauty to follow to the next
Review your action of demeanor daily
And if need be-take charge to modify a balancing and intricate text
A window or visual gateway of a never-ending world of perfection of the above
Catering into the promised land is the actual goal of my personal testimony
I hope that you don't tap into any reservation to locate a nagging negative
Because the forever is real and not understood as being phony
Forever paradise or the greatest claim to live always
110% better than earthly great
I pray the you choose with free agency-it is choice that claims as never late
Where you are viewed as an ethereal angel and you do your job
Entertaining angels we all have done unknowingly
For me-it is obvious as I earn my heavenly and sacred degree
Never growing old
A fable with parable attached...
Time to tame the demons-my story will be told
I observe your actions and admire you...
For you are not weak and actually quite bold
Would you like a temporary glimpse at what lay beyond?
I know accurately this may not make sense
But when you get there it is like a billion or more smiles
And joy itself-is greater than a zillion credentials-never tripped up as dense
We all have had both pain and sorrow
But believe that Jehovah and his perfect son's death on the cross
It is now time to reshuffle the cards in the deck
…Work for the King-call Him the Almighty boss
It is never too late-save the lost-a societal wreck
The immortal portal
Try
Hollering from way out and quite far
Learn to pray for others and even you
Substantially put
Endure to the end only to see it thru
Check your desk and stick around as if super glue

WRITTEN BY:BRIAN MOILANEN-2024

The meaning of life

I talk to my soul
I scream at my conscious
And debate with my brain
As my mind accepts the chore at hand
A trying moment that in time we will all command
Who and what calls the shots
A systemic proportion of luck and ability
That although unique is like comparing video games to merely robots
A new world
A special touch
Healing right now is taking place
A paralyzed human absorbed without the need for a crutch
Give and taking
Taking and giving
Survival meets it beginning
And pleasure is acquired by those upright and proper living
Spoke with a child tyrant of immense winning
A 4.0 complete scholastic honor is what he obtained
Yet he is certain areas was uniquely obsessed with gentle caress of sinning
No need for weed
No need for smoke
A drink from the Holy challis
Is quite possibly what this tidbit of information spells-I interpret and evoke
The God of all gods stands true and firm
If you do or don't agree
Is not in contention-although timelines sometimes suppress
Do we understand?
Is that guiding light of light there to confess?
Confession and doxology is there to bless
We all need a rest
Am I winning this contest?
I pray and pray alike
I peddle up a never-ending hill
But what or whom confuses this as an obliged soul at rest?
The meaning of life
A modern ice age is becoming to maybe be true
A colossal infusion propelled with an equation of test versus strife
Kids at home with an ensemble of what we must do
My foot fits the mold
But am I sure that I am possibly one of the chosen few?
Some days never appear to begin
So darn much
I play cards with angels and spirits intervening against what is vile
The segue of even a tin man who does become chagrin
A thousand meanings to the purpose of life
It will change always
As we embrace our fate
Balancing destiny of free will versus fate
It all causes me to see what is truly irate
WRITTEN BY:BRIAN MOILANEN-2023

Thinking back on yesterday

Today is merely yesterdays tomorrow
Are you well acquainted with joyous heart?
Or as a matter of fact filled with sorrow?
My mind becomes and gets torn in two
Harvesting all this madness
And as I see it-maybe all this is just a human zoo
Sometimes I cling to my feelings
Other times you know-It is difficult to just redo
Back into the action of all of those yesterdays
Concert like life footage
As my tendency holds to that of being within acting in plays
Furthermore I must add this time it is seen and observed as charades
Are you an actor?
Or simply phased as a reactor?
Remembrance
Independence
Toys from my past
Can't you remember what you did a year ago?
I feel as if a boat trapped on a frigid sea of madness
I feel my inner drive alive although and as an amber igniting the fire
Watch me kindle and with fiery orange clatter just glow
I miss the memories of yesterday
I bet that you do too
I attempt to put together this walk down memory lane
Because forthright I have grown and likewise also grew
And if my past logic and memories hold their weight
Hopscotching with just one leg not forget to mention just one shoe
Photo albums
Passed letters
I observe all of this going into a grand understanding of the term recollection
I lead with my heart
And gather with my soul the value of true fun
A feather so to say that weighs about one ton
I have moved out of the rain and fog
Directly into this beautiful and shining yellow sun
Gather your thoughts
Collect upon your eternal and external mind
All you have given
And all that you did find
I'm not the toughest of cookies
But yet from there on also not the weakest
The question of importance is to remember to simply say...please
I don't intend to venture into the past all day long
But I feel as free as a bird
Warbling with virtue and also with angelic soft song
All is said
All is done
I stand still and in place
While my emotions just run

WRITTEN BY:Brian Moilanen-2022

Touching an angel

Angels will find you with everlasting beautified kisses
They hopefully are pulling you out of a sickening scary and burning hell
Others call this the bottomless pit and vile abysses
Touching an angel
A last attempt to save another soul
The world is running from sins and iniquities
Spoken in metaphor the burning of charred burned black coal
Save a soul
Care and love compete as being that of one
Harvesting within the today eons of endless time
A win the Almighty gathers yet the work henceforth is never done
Believe in the self
Believe ultimately in the King
Harmony of brilliance and everlasting light joins this calling
Angels on high continue at their best praise to adore and sing
Is the world's end of days drawing near? Or is Jehovah presently stalling?
A new heaven
A new earth
A new way
a cherubs birth
The Armageddon draws close
Swallow the medications that relief with dote a communion of souls
Believe if you will my understanding that's true
We did not come from apes or lack of gravity being that of black holes
The new beginning of all new beginnings is not far off
Most agree
As for the stubborn they only scoff
Three crosses
Three wishes
Three holy choices
Forthright just one decision
Good logistics marvel for those who aim to overcome
From master to slave or even a panhandling bum
Focus with the good book
Abide to follow the Scriptures of ten
A question of when
I blot out sins for the lost as to enter into heaven
Another name describes love with black the ink of the pen
Thank God
Thank You

WRITTEN BY: BRIAN MOILANEN-2020

Twisted together

You look at me
Extremely compounded I stare back at you
We take sides and hear each other again
This is crazy as we combined together as if super glue
Deep hearts
Awkward instance begs our souls
Just like throwing darts
We watch as the dice thrown ventures and quickly rolls
Twisted together
Tangled hearts
Two tons of feathers
And not sure of the ends or even the starts
Perpetual madness
Or is it confusion in hand?
Decreasing becomes my emotion-infiltrated sadness
Pebbles increase and complete this dirt and sand
I love you, at least for this day
Maybe this will make sense
I stop and decide to make this meaningful sense
I stop and pray
Now for once I just do not know-although why I am tense
Sometimes musing emotions
And other times I need a souls release
Add up the options
Only to find an inner peace
Oil the rusted tires
And watch the car run better and not cease
Or add an alternate help as with a gooey grease
Stuck together
Becoming uniquely put all in one
The balance of nature
Equates both work and also fun
Super glue
Rubber bands
Scotch tape
A rebuttal of interest along with what importance of prayer demands
It is now ultimately your call
Stand or fall?
Be on time
And like playing poker learn just when to pass or stall
Do not quit
Okay-you can quit
But if you do
I bet that you will only blatantly sit
It is time to decide
Grab the wheel and continue to ride

WRITTEN BY:BRIAN MOILANEN 2022

113

Two ton feathers

Homage to my ancestors
And all included-like wise to anybody else that are of family
Personal growth accelerates through and with lineage
Welcome now in heaven to your exalted family tree
Language of the god's comes to me more abundant now-thanks for the coverage
Loved ones that we didn't have a chance to formally meet
Manage and learn to grow now with complete knowledge
At times an extensive balancing act
Remember that with every periled or advantaged action
Comes forthright a reaction
Two ton feathers
Pray for the weak
Henceforth pray for those strong
Light and dark
Dark and light
In the waving winds flies
A little child's kite
Yet thunder hits as if a ton of bricks
A gray area so to say
With every decision also comes the challenging conflict
Strange observation of twist of plot
Chance with chance circumstance is also ironic
Some claim those hit with overcoming more than need be
Pave a newer path not of the negative attribute
They only need to be finally set free
They more times than not also do see
Do your unending homework
And witness firsthand that the trivializing skeptics now do agree
Aim for the light
Or aim for the dark
Aim for the God given gifts of all and too all
So braggers believe to conceive that they
Are also likewise not bracketed in any area-from very small to increasingly tall
Some judge
While others for example
Only detain
See the glowing yellow sunshine
With the falling crystal wet drops of soothing rain
I know
In many ways I too have learned
And proceeding into doing my best
I also have earned
The latter stages have progressed and
Have weighed for the sake of weighing-have yearned

Waiting within the shadows

Waiting
And even more waiting
Within the shadows
My brain as if it could bleed-as my heart is perspiring
Seeking to find a better day-uniquely although I realize I am not alone
Flipping thru a magazine-certain articles and pictures evolve as inspiring
Yet I am feeling slightly better-my self worth alters and does improve
A disposition of sweet sentiment overcomes me-not weak and tiring
Waiting within the shadows
I count my friends while ignoring my foes
Do you take lead with the chin
Or do you engage with the problematic governed by your own nose
Because although we live by the choices we make
Does serendipity alone raise the ante?
And we all can be vulnerable and just must release the soul and freely take
I feel like at times a fast track gazelle running from the preying cheetah
The fields of a beige and green environment seem to keep up with the chase
Yet the gazelle stands firm and fully alive and has passed another test
Life compared to a juggling act within nature-survive at prayer and individual pace
All have conjured magic thru prayer as even more than the Pastor has taught and confessed
Furthermore no life is so short
That things can't take on a newer positive change
Comparing my life to a jigsaw puzzle-I do not know it seems currently as misleading purport
Never as of now stay the same-wow things just fall into place and rearrange
I will add take a chance
Yet please-yes please-do not burn a bridge
New stuff to encounter
Life a test for all-from machine to man- to animal-to even a simple gold fish
Be sure to pass the challis
And try your best to tithe that of 10% at the donation and tithing plate or dish
I read and study and must add with change of ways truly do cram
My heart strings are getting plucked gradually
And open a margin as that being a crustacean deep sea clam
A time to give
Other times I must take take
God created all-yes all-from bird to spiders and even the dove and snake
A Richter scale of nearly 9.0 hits this softened heart that of a shaking rapid earthquake
No longer will I allow myself for toil and forsake
Life is now-powerful and what I create and of it make

WRITTEN BY: BRIAN MOILANEN-2020

When mental illness strikes

When mental illness strikes
Yet not quite sure of the time or date
As my nuances trigger vivid observation at full tilt
Subjected by and without what appears as quite irate
Schizophrenia terrorizes most persons in its path
Often times its victims although will take a purifying bath
Mercy guides as mercy also does endure
Not speaking oddly
But I realize when living is good the days and times often do blur
Mental illness is not a fault of my own
I pay homage to my personal Saviour
If this material is evident
Then onward I move and therefore I am sure
Is this a symbol of purity?
That shines light no matter what comes-anyhow and anyway
My heart beats in cadence
My soul goes to shine and is brought about to morally play
DNA and RNA seem to make evidently-a lot of sense
Spirituality engulfs to take more of being in charge
Destiny prays
Destiny plays
Destiny appeals as it also displays
A host of hosts bring all that it weighs
Hmm...A hocus-pocus approach that compiles in many versatile ways
Locate quite accurately a method to overcome
The wise old adage is true and often times just won't lose
I advise you to not fall off the bandwagon and become a transient bum
Pain is felt
Pain often times is also dealt
Never did I want this disease
I pray upon my bowed knees
Choose to win
Wins and losses
Smile in zealous behaviour
In hopes of eventually with our Saviour
True enough today there is not a cure
Don't hold your breath is what I will confess to
Getting nearer to a method for the madness
I am not formed from a cookie curter so to say
The awkwardness is looming once again
My feelings with emotions I hope are going northbound
Accurate knowledge
Wisdom gathers as is with intelligence
And not flying south
Do not give in
Do not let loose
Drink from the Holy Challis
As you drink the wine in testimony of our dear Lord

WRITTEN BY:BRIAN MOILANEN-2023

When the vivid days begin to blur

When the vivid days begin to blur
It becomes engrossed within the evident
And occasionally becomes a snare guided within the obscure
What in my life is going just right?
And what in my life is going just wrong?
Eternal desires are often bred
So much to mention
Yet on the other hand
So much has been left unsaid
A good day on this earth
Or a day where I would be at a finished greeting-so long;for I am now dead
Try not to complain if the days seem quite long
For the day will come you are no longer here
And another world shall welcome you
Possibly a vastness of entertainment or...better yet a heavenly plan
Time is before, now, and always with us
The sunshine filters as not too burn us yet a super imposed Godly span
Take time for hobbies as of new
Trying to manufacture if you will adhesives that in origin all begin as glue
Get on the good foot
And make sure that you have the correct sandal or shoe
We all must stand the test of time
At times our situation in life may appear as rough
Mountains and hills to climb
But I believe that I have the correct stuff
A juggling act
And further more-where are your emotions?
I speak on interest of...what is fallacy and what is fact?
Seize the day
Or so goes this cliché
A reference of dimensions withdrawn from space and time
Not forget to mention measurements of a brain with ease
And for that matter the ease of questions of bounty pure
Am I wrong?
Am I right?
Will I lose yet still engaged within this paradox
I at least have my intentions and seek to...at least try what's right
Do not give up
Do not give in
Do not destroy
If you aim to alter and pass again within the bridge
Use your time wisely
For this time is all that you technically have
Repair the cut and abrasion on your brain
So much effort
So much strain
For now I am ready to sign off
Best of luck
I tried to shed some light
So please, please, see my deeds are well and need not scoff

WRITTEN BY:BRIAN MOILANEN-2022

Where have those days gone?
Time-sometimes it goes so slow

On the opposite end of the spectrum sometimes it goes so fast

I live my best according to my situation

And I pray that my Lord sees me as having passed

Every day that passes occasionally we have an opportunity to see more of this creation

Yet where does time go to?

Where have those days gone?

Most believe that we had our forming from God Almighty and angel divine

We are all included and it becomes obvious to see this sign

Do you know what I am getting at?

Does this now all become relevant?

An angel given is also a special angel sent

Praying for forgiveness

And putting it into practice in layman's terms

Is the definition of the word…repent

No one is perfect

We are all human

The bobble is quickly popped

As we all do sin

Some days are full of times to cherish as we venture into memory lane

Get involved in the innocence of justice and retribution of

The birds fly in the heavens and not forget to mention also the blue skies above

The bird of peace is a fancy for some and it is understood as the holy dove

Who knows you may communicate from your mind along with your soul

Unity and contentment will take you far

For you are the only you made

Not within the orchestra of power you become the lasting star

WRITTEN BY: BRIAN MOILANEN-2022

WORDS

WORDS CAN BOOST AND WORDS CAN BREAK

A FRIEND FOR ALL SO WHAT IS ON THE TAKE?

SOMETIME I GIVE AND OTHER TIMES I FORSAKE

ARE YOU ALIVE AND FULLY AWAKE?

SOME DAYS ARE GOOD AND OTHERS ARE NOT

A BATTLE WON

IS A BATTLE FOUGHT

A LESSON LEARNED

IS A LESSON TAUGHT

DO NOT GIVE IN

AND THEREFORE DO NOT QUIT

WHEN TO STAND

AND WHEN TO SIT

WORDS ADD AND WORDS SUBTRACT

TRUTH OF KNOWLEDGE IS A FACT

LOVE KEEPS US ALL TOGETHER AT THE SEEMS

QUALITY OF INSTANCE

A SUBTLE GLOW IS MORE THAN INTENSE

THE SUNSHINE IN THE HEAVENS IS BRIGHT AND TROPICALLY DENSE

MAKE A CONGENIAL EFFORT TO PLEASE THOSE THAT PLEASE YOU

DONE, DID AND DO

IF THE FOOT FITS THE SHOE

YOU HAVE LANDED QUITE POSSIBLY IN A HUMAN ZOO

WRITTEN BY: BRIAN MOILANEN 2022

You can't refund yesterday

Just how to spend my time?
Universal memories in which this mind accurately manifests in which too hold
Is this a fable or even that of a legend of consistency attributed rhyme
Yet also must I add that I will journey in which to implore
Explore
Peek around the corner to sneak a peak
My words are legitimate and the message will not ever abhor
Feeling and sending messages divine and allowing time also to tweak
Crash course in religion is that a spirited earthly number is #4
Given and not being able to be taken away-unprecedented and forthright
Blind one's without sight
Now do begin to see
A pleasant delight
Anchored in the ocean's turf and at current on my wispy boat
Compelled clearly into peace and not fists engaged into fight
Waves tumble and crash yet I strangely enough clear my throat
Is it possible to reverse the cards which now have a profusion of sight
Do not worry or ever take a nod of self defeating gloat
You can"t refund yesterday
Live within the today
You can't refund yesterday
Wipe the slate clean-my own personal way
Pictures and images of the illustrious past come to mind
Going and moving forward
And only momentarily getting stuck in the rewind
We I know all have gaunt weaknesses
But realize that I have penance and aim to settle the score
Treat others as you wish to be treated
Betting and raising the ante this much is true
I am not a bragging man or enveloped within arrogance or even conceited
Hmm...time
A component or card that we all do hold
Impact evident
I find uniquely enough although I was the book that rarely sold
Play your cards-or they may just play you
Onward moving soldiers remain both courageous and bold
Yet acknowledging infinity begins now-just what is the unprecedented curfew?
A balancing act that disciplines and also has obtained three fold
Stay safe always
And remain forthright to get shelter from the frigid cold

WRITTEN BY:BRIAN MOILANEN-2020

Your contribution left unnoticed

Your contribution left sadly unnoticed
Association with an image
I dug in heals but still I just missed
Touching the clouds with more than just one wish
The sun shines as I gave the best just to have kissed
Flying high being an opponent of injustice and lies
Am I right?
Do you firmly agree?
Play your cards wisely and close to the chest
A feeling obtained with kind gesture and also Christ like words
A battle that if claimed as a comforting soul
Is a statement in which I have been as high as the birds
And my heart is now free and at grounds for parole
This world is tough and difficult
Be exact if you will
Over much heartache as good guides a path of a result
You must not give in and move forward to try
Observations are accurate
My stance in life is not to deny
If requested-contact me with directions to ordain as meaning to comply
Angels and saints
Emotions won't conflict
Within a preponderance that is glowing and also a gem that is round
Meeting this understanding as being more than accurate
And always to be found
Inherited heaven a meaning that believers who trigger all good-just cant stop
And are seen as being in more than the hear-and-now
Substantial differences of the end of all wars is near
The end is running rampant and uniquely very near
The end has begun
The battle for heaven
And passages of the Holy Bible are noted from a spiritual seer
Providing light and prayers that will improve
A challenging course
Seeking for mercy to just aprove
Believe in a higher power
Also known to some as good orderly direction
This war called the Armageddon-shall one day cease
Once again free a soul
See the prophets role will win and shall increase
Put on the best display of holy and great
A God that is good and starts early-so never to be late
WRITTEN BY:BRIAN MOILANEN-2023

Zebra crosses

Consequently I now see more of this zebra cross tradition
The worlds prayers and the like-wise are focused upon the above
So please deny the human failings of underlying suspicion
Sisters and brothers-most have sight
Yet sometimes the path detours from neglect and omission
Out of the dense jungle-and even farther from the tethered woods
An altered ego demises from sensation of Godly praise and ambition
Zebra crosses
So to say that of a balancing act
The soul and spirit universally have combined to any overt losses
A dark knight
Feeling beaten and sometimes cries
Misunderstood yet obtaining what I define as congenial
Turn maybe even to theism and efforts of if society denies
Planning that is humble and even menial
Better yet aim to locate a form of grateful love
Pathways to intentions of symbolism now fly high a warbling dove
Without understanding
The spirited heart shines from within
Today virtues are in the skies-and angels we all see with a delivered grin
Some prudent as their characters say...why?
At the least-Bye God-maybe thru conscience we all have been
Or maybe not
A lesson learned is a lesson taught
Another battle with the pen being mightier than the sword
God is in my ring also-And for me it is the King who has fought
Do your best
Set the marker high
Don't edge God out
Or in other words confidently seek to abolish your ego and please comply
Happy medium
Yet likewise never let down your guard
Remember that evil is what God should and will have feathered and tarred
Change your ways
It is not too late
Marveling and marvelous integrity
Behind closed doors do the right thing
Walk by faith and not by sight-maybe learn this guarantee
Don't sweat the small stuff
Furthermore...do you agree?
Your call...Will you put forth the effort for all eternity

WRITTEN BY:BRIAN MOILANEN-2020